The Christian Book of Mystical Verse

The Christian Book
of
Mystical Verse

by

A.W. Tozer

MOCKINGBIRD
PRESS

Copyright © 2022 Mockingbird Press

All rights reserved. The original works are in the public domain to the best of publisher's knowledge. The publisher makes no claim to the original writings. However, the compilation, construction, cover design, trademarks, derivations, foreword, descriptions, added work, etc., of this edition are copyrighted and may not be reproduced, distributed, or transmitted in any form or by any means, including photocopying, recording, or other electronic or mechanical methods, without the prior written permission of the publisher, except in the case of brief quotations embodied in critical reviews and certain other non-commercial uses permitted by copyright law, or where content is specifically noted as being reproduced under a Creative Commons license.

Cover, "Teich am Abend," by Christian Rohlfs, 1896
Foreword, Copyright © 2022 Mockingbird Press, LLC
Cover Design by Matthew Johnson, Copyright © 2022 Mockingbird Press, LLC
Interior Design by Daria Lacy

Publisher's Cataloging-In-Publication Data

Tozer, A.W., author; with Underhill, Rachael, Foreword by
The Christian Book of Mystical Verse / A.W. Tozer; with Rachael Underhill

Paperback	ISBN-13: 978-1-68493-015-9
Hardback	ISBN-13: 978-1-68493-016-6
Ebook	ISBN-13: 978-1-68493-017-3

1. Religion—Christian Living—General. 2. Philosophy & Religion—Religion & Beliefs—Christianity—Christian Life & Practice, I. A.W. Tozer. II. Rachael Underhill. III. The Christian Book of Mystical Verse.

REL012000 / QRMP

Type Set in Century Schoolbook / **Franklin Gothic Demi**

Mockingbird Press, Augusta, GA
info@mockingbirdpress.com

Contents

Foreword ix

Adoration Of The Godhead 5
    Eternal Power! 5
    Lord Of All Being 6
    Adoration 6
    The Unity Of God 7
    The Holy Trinity 8
    Majesty Divine! 10
    The Vision Of The Godhead 12
    The Thought Of God 14
    The Greatness Of God 16
    The Eternity Of God 18
    The Fear Of God 20
    The Eternal Father 22
    The Eternal Generation Of The Son 24
    The Holy Spirit 26
    Pentecost 28

Devotional Meditations On The Cross Of Christ 31
    If Sweet The Moments, Rich In Blessing 31
    Ride On! Ride On In Majesty! 32
    Would Jesus Have The Sinner Die? 32
    He Dies! The Friend Of Sinners Dies! 34
    Before The Cross 35
    O Sacred Head, Now Wounded 35
    Not All The Blood Of Beasts 36

Penitential Reflections On Our Sins 39
    My Sins, My Saviour! 39
    Have Mercy, God Most High 40
    O Lord, I Am Ashamed To Seek Thy Face 41
    Scourge, But Receive Me 42

Rejoicing In Forgiveness And Justification 43
Song Of Assurance 43
A Good Confession 44
A Soul In Its Earliest Love 45

Yearning For Purity Of Heart 47
I Thirst, Thou Wounded Lamb Of God 47
Prayer For Purity 48
Jesus, Thine All-Victorious Love 49
Self-Love 50

Aspirations After God 53
As Pants The Hart 53
The Way Of Perfection 54
Thou Shepherd Of Israel, And Mine 55
The Fervor Of Holy Desire 56
Desire Of God 57
Satisfied 59

Delighting In God's Presence 61
God Is Present Everywhere 61
The Royal Priesthood 62
God Reveals His Presence 62
Within The Holy Place 63
Lo, God Is Here! 64
Allured Into The Desert 64

The Raptures Of Divine Love 67
O Love Divine! 67
I Love My God 68
The Acquiescence Of Pure Love 68
Jesus, Thy Boundless Love To Me 69
O Love Divine! 70
The Hidden Love Of God 71
Love's Immensity 72

The Rest Of Faith **73**
  All Must Be Well 73
  Confidence 74
  Sometimes A Light Surprises 75
  The Blessed Journey 75
  Jesus, I Am Resting, Resting 76
  Resignation 77
  In Heavenly Love Abiding 78
  The Remembrance Of Mercy 79

The Spiritual Warfare **81**
  Distractions In Prayer 81
  The Benefits Of Suffering 83
  Sorrow And Love 84

Victory Through Praise **85**
  Come, O My Soul 85
  Bless, O My Soul, The Living God 86
  I'll Praise My Maker 86
  I Sing Th' Almighty Power Of God 87
  Now Thank We All Our God 88
  Te Deum Laudamus 89

The Prayer Of Quiet **91**
  The Spirit Of Prayer 91
  My God! Silent To Thee! 91
  God's Eternal Now 92
  My Heart Is Resting, O My God 93
  Hidden In God's Heart 94

The Bliss Of Communion **95**
  The Disciple To His Lord 95
  Joy In The Presence Of Jesus 96
  O Jesus, King Most Wonderful 97
  Christ Our Light 97
  As Ointment Poured Forth 98

O! Tell Me, Thou Life And Delight Of My Soul! 99
The Face Of Christ 100
Christ, Whose Glory Fills The Skies 100
Jesu, Highest Heaven's Completeness 101
Show Me Thy Face 101
None Other Lamb, None Other Name 102
Aspirations Of The Soul After Christ 103
The Pain Of Love 104
Thou Hidden Source Of Calm Repose 105
The Man Divine 106
Thee Will I Love 107
At The Lord's Table 109
Prayer Before Communion 110
The Indwelling Christ 110
As Incense Streaming Forth 111
Hosanna, Lord! 112
Am I Not Enough? 113
Jesus, Thou Joy Of Loving Hearts 113

Joyous Anticipation Of Christ's Return 115
Wake, Awake, For Night Is Flying 115
Lo! He Comes! 116
The Hope Of His Coming 118
The Blessed Morrow 118

Immortality And The World To Come 121
Lift Your Glad Voices 121
Jesus Lives, And So Shall I 121
O Sing Hallelujah! 123
Those Endless Sabbaths 124
In Immanuel's Land 124
The Celestial Country 129

Notes 141

Foreword

The *Christian Book of Mystical Verse*, first published in 1963, is a collection of poems, hymns, and prayers compiled by Christian pastor and writer A.W. Tozer. Intended to provide an aid to the devotee, it is a selection of over 100 pieces of theologically sound verse to support "the worshipping soul."

A.W. Tozer (1897-1963) was a self-educated pastor. He first heard the call to Christianity as a teen, when he heard a street preacher say, "If you don't know how to be saved ... just call on God, saying 'Lord be merciful to me a sinner.'" Tozer heeded the call, and began a life dedicated to Christ.

Calling on God became a cornerstone of his faith. He had an intensely personal relationship with God, and was seen to pray in his office for hours at a time, sometimes on his couch and sometimes prostrate on the floor. As a pastor with the Christian and Missionary Alliance, he spent his career preaching Biblical doctrine, advocating that his congregants turn away from worldliness and toward the fundamentals of the faith.

Tozer also wrote prolifically, completing 12 books on theology, as well as innumerable essays and articles for magazines like *Alliance Weekly* and *Christian Life*.

It may seem odd to find a fundamentalist like Tozer use the word "mystical" in the title of his collection. But in his introduction, he differentiates the Christian mystic from those with "a strong psychic bent that predisposes them toward the occult ... ready to accept whatever in the realm of religion is bizarre and prodigious."

Rather, the mystic of Tozer's collection had experienced "... that personal spiritual experience common to the saints of Bible times and well known to multitudes of persons in the post-Biblical era. I refer to the evangelical mystic who has been brought by the gospel into intimate fellowship with the Godhead." Those he identified as mystics include clergy and pastors, hymn writers, poets, reformers, and others.

They span different denominations of Christianity, from French Roman Catholics to German Calvinists to American Baptists.

To Tozer, the mystical is God-oriented. The poems in his collection "...begin with God, embrace the worshipping soul and return to God again." While these verses are not from the scriptures, one can trust that they are fully supported by the Biblical text. A fundamentalist like Tozer would not include any hymn or prayer that was not theologically sound and supported by the source material.

There are 111 verses and hymns included in this collection, divided into 15 logical sections:

1. Adoration of the Godhead
2. Devotional Meditations on the Cross of Christ
3. Penitential Reflections on Our Sins
4. Rejoicing in Forgiveness and Justification
5. Yearning for Purity of Heart
6. Aspirations After God
7. Delighting in God's Presence
8. The Raptures of Divine Love
9. The Rest of Faith
10. The Spiritual Warfare
11. Victory Through Praise
12. The Prayer of Quiet
13. The Bliss of Communion
14. Joyous Anticipation of Christ's Return
15. Immortality and the World to Come

As Tozer explains, "This is a book for the worshiper rather than for the student...Everything here is for use in private devotion. I have had in mind not a congregation but the lone individual." The collection can be used as a devotional, with the reader meditating on a single verse each day. The organization by topic can also let you search for verses that will support your current Bible study. Or, simply flip to a page at random, and see which verse has been chosen for you on that day.

The *Christian Book of Mystical Verse* was the last of Tozer's books to be published during his lifetime. Since then, many more compilations of his essays, sermons, and articles have been published, ensuring that this brilliant Christian is still being read and enjoyed by modern audiences.

INTRODUCTION

The purpose of this book is to bring together in one convenient volume some of the best devotional verse the English language affords, and thus to make available to present day Christians a rich spiritual heritage which the greater number of them for various reasons do not now enjoy.

I have not hesitated to apply the term "mystical" to the material I have collected here, though I readily admit that fewer than half a dozen of the men and women who would be called true mystics in the strict classical sense will be found here. Such names as Eckhart, Ruysbroeck, John of the Cross, Teresa, Rolle, Tauler, Hilton, Francis of Assisi, for instance, are not represented in this volume at all. On the other hand the frequent appearance of such a man as Watts might cause the reader to lift a questioning eyebrow and ask, "Is Watts also among the mystics?"

Well, the answer must be, Of course he is, and so are John Newton and James Montgomery and Reginald Heber and Charles Wesley, as well as many others who might have balked at being called mystics but whose writings, nevertheless, reveal unmistakable traces of purest mysticism and are the better for it. And for that matter the same thing may be said of the inspired writings of such men as Moses and David and Isaiah and Daniel and Paul and John, the works of the latter showing more than traces of the mystical spirit, being indeed charged full with it.

As short a time as, say, forty years ago, the words "mystic" and "mystical" were altogether unacceptable in evangelical circles. Among the gospel churches the words suggested someone who was emotionally unstable, visionary, and worst of all, unsound theologically.

Now there are undoubtedly many persons with a temperamental fondness for the fantastic. These have by nature a strong psychic bent that predisposes them toward the occult; they have also an incredible capacity for self-deception and are ready to accept whatever in the realm of religion is bizarre and prodigious. Such as these have been sometimes called mystics—something they most surely are not.

The word "mystic" as it occurs in the title of this book refers to that personal spiritual experience common to the saints of Bible times and well known to multitudes of persons in the post-Biblical era. I refer to the evangelical mystic who has been brought by the gospel into intimate fellowship with the Godhead. His theology is no less and no more than is taught in the Christian Scriptures. He walks the high road of truth where walked of old prophets and apostles, and where down the centuries walked martyrs, reformers, Puritans, evangelists and missionaires of the cross. He differs from the ordinary orthodox Christian only because he experiences his faith down in the depths of his sentient being while the other does not. He exists in a world of spiritual reality. He is quietly, deeply, and sometimes almost ecstatically aware of the Presence of God in his own nature and in the world around him. His religious experience is something elemental, as old as time and the creation. It is immediate acquaintance with God by union with the Eternal Son. It is to know that which passes knowledge.

The hymns and poems found here are mystical in that they are God-oriented; they begin with God, embrace the worshipping soul and return to God again. And they cover almost the full spectrum of religious feeling: fear, hope, penitence, aspiration, the longing to be holy, yearning after God, gratitude, thanksgiving, pure admiration of the Godhead, love for Christ, worship, praise and adoration. The mood runs from near despair to near ecstasy, and the twin notes of utter sincerity and deepest reverence may be heard throughout.

This is a book for the worshiper rather than, for the student. It has been carefully and lovingly prepared for those God-enamored persons who, while they feel as deeply as the enraptured poet, yet lack the gift that would enable them to express their feelings adequately. Such will sense a kinship with the gifted souls they find on the pages of this book and will join them as they mount on high to pour out their hymns at heaven's gate.

In making these selections I have largely followed my own bent, though I have been guided somewhat by a few simple rules. First, all sentimental verse was excluded, along with everything homey and maudlin. The only healthy emotions are those aroused by great ideas, and even these must be restrained and purified by the Spirit of God or they will spend themselves in weak and sterile rhymes. Of such there is enough in the religious world; I think none will be found in this book.

Second, while the compiler is not unfamiliar with the judgment of hymnologists and literary critics on the larger body of English religious verse, that judgment has been set aside and another adopted for this book. For this reason some of the standard classics have been omitted because I felt they would not contribute to my purpose. Conversely, certain poems of admittedly inferior literary rank have been included because I felt that they would.

Third, everything selected for inclusion in this work had to be judged theologically sound. While considerable latitude was allowed, even welcomed, in doctrinal outlook and emphasis, to be accepted every hymn and poem had to meet the test of faithfulness to the Christian Scriptures.

Though almost everything here is pure lyric poetry and may easily be sung, yet this book is not intended for use in the public assembly. Had I meant it to be so used a wholly different kind of verse would have been chosen for it and the book would have been another sort of book altogether. Everything here is for use in private devotion. I have had in mind not a congregation but the lone individual. For this reason I would respectfully urge the one who may come into possession of this book not to "read" it as he would read another book. Let him try rather to enter into its mood, to capture and be captured by its spirit. How many pages he gets through in a day is of no importance; what one poem or even one single stanza does to him and for him and in him: that is everything.

Admittedly much pure gold has been left out of this treasury. The chief reason is lack of space. I have tried to keep the book small enough to be portable, that its possessor may carry it with him and so turn any bus or train or airplane into a sanctuary. Certainly not all the gold in the world is in this one volume, but what is here is, I believe, true gold of Ophir. I hope many of my fellow Christians will find it to be so.

A. W. Tozer

ADORATION OF THE GODHEAD

ETERNAL POWER!

Eternal Power, whose high abode
Becomes the grandeur of a God:
Infinite lengths beyond the bounds
Where stars revolve their little rounds:

Thee while the first archangel sings,
He hides his face behind his wings:
And ranks of shining thrones around
Fall worshipping, and spread the ground.

Lord, what shall earth and ashes do?
We would adore our Maker too;
From sin and dust to Thee we cry,
The Great, the Holy, and the High.

Earth, from afar, hath heard Thy fame,
And worms have learn'd to lisp Thy Name;
But O! the glories of Thy mind
Leave all our soaring thoughts behind.

God is in heaven, and men below:
Be short our times; our words be few:
A solemn reverence checks our songs,
And praise sits silent on our tongues.

—*Isaac Watts, 1674-1748*

LORD OF ALL BEING

Lord of all being, throned afar,
Thy glory flames from sun and star;
Center and soul of every sphere,
Yet to each loving heart how near.

Sun of our life, Thy quickening ray
Sheds on our path the glow of day;
Star of our hope, Thy softened light
Cheers the long watches of the night.

Our midnight is Thy smile withdrawn;
Our noontide is Thy gracious dawn;
Our rainbow arch, Thy mercy's sign;
All, save the clouds of sin, are Thine.

Lord of all life, below, above,
Whose light is truth, whose warmth is love,
Before Thy ever blazing throne
We ask no luster of our own.

Grant us Thy truth to make us free,
And kindling hearts that burn for Thee,
Till all Thy living altars claim
One holy light, one heavenly flame.

—*Oliver Wendell Holmes, 1809-1894*

ADORATION

Almighty One! I bend in dust before Thee;
Even so veiled cherubs bend;
In calm and still devotion I adore Thee,
All-wise, all-present Friend!

Thou to the earth its emerald robes hast given,
Or curtained it in snow;
And the bright sun, and the soft moon in heaven,
Before Thy presence bow.

Thou Power sublime! whose throne is firmly seated
On stars and glowing suns;
O, could I praise Thee,—could my soul, elated,
Waft Thee seraphic tones, —
Had I the lyres of angels, —could I bring Thee
An offering worthy Thee, —
In what bright notes of glory would I sing Thee,
Blest notes of ecstasy!

Eternity! Eternity! how solemn,
How terrible the sound!
Here, leaning on thy promises, —a column
Of strength, —may I be found,
O, let my heart be ever Thine, while beating,
As when 'twill cease to beat!
Be Thou my portion, till that awful meeting
When I my God shall greet!

—*Sir John Bowring, 1792-1872*

THE UNITY OF GOD

One God! one Majesty!
There is no God but Thee!
Unbounded, unextended Unity!

Awful in unity,
O God! we worship Thee,
More simply one, because supremely Three!

Dread, unbeginning One!
Single, yet not alone,
Creation hath not set Thee on a higher throne.

Unfathomable Sea!
All life is out of Thee,
And Thy life is Thy blissful Unity.

All things that from Thee run,
All works that Thou hast done,
Thou didst in honour of Thy being One.

And by Thy being One,
Ever by that alone,
Couldst Thou do, and doest, what Thou hast done.

We from Thy oneness come,
Beyond it cannot roam,
And in Thy oneness find our one eternal home.

Blest be Thy Unity!
All joys are one to me,—
The joy that there can be no other God than Thee!

—Frederick William Faber, 1814-1863

THE HOLY TRINITY

O Blessed Trinity!
Thy children dare to lift their hearts to Thee,
And bless Thy triple Majesty!
Holy Trinity!
Blessed Equal Three,
One God, we praise Thee.

O Blessed Trinity!
Holy, unfathomable, infinite,
Thou art all Life and Love and Light.
Holy Trinity!
Blessed Equal Three,
One God, we praise Thee.

O Blessed Trinity!
God of a thousand attributes! we see
That there is no one good but Thee.
Holy Trinity!
Blessed Equal Three,
One God, we praise Thee.

O Blessed Trinity!
In our astonished reverence we confess
Thine uncreated loveliness.
Holy Trinity!
Blessed Equal Three,
One God, we praise Thee.

O Blessed Trinity!
O simplest Majesty! O Three in One!
Thou art for ever God alone.
Holy Trinity!
Blessed Equal Three,
One God, we praise Thee.

O Blessed Trinity!
The Fountain of the Godhead, in repose,
For ever rests, for ever flows.
Holy Trinity!
Blessed Equal Three,
One God, we praise Thee.

O Blessed Trinity!
O Unbegotten Father! give us tears
To quench our love, to calm our fears.
Holy Trinity!
Blessed Equal Three,
One God, we praise Thee.

O Blessed Trinity!
Bright Son! who art the Father's mind displayed,
Thou art begotten and not made.
Holy Trinity!
Blessed Equal Three,
One God, we praise Thee.

O Blessed Trinity!
Coequal Spirit! wondrous Paraclete!
By Thee the Godhead is complete.
Holy Trinity!
Blessed Equal Three,
One God, we praise Thee.

O Blessed Trinity!
We praise Thee, bless Thee, worship Thee as one.
Yet Three are on the single Throne.
Holy Trinity!
Blessed Equal Three,
One God, we praise Thee.

O Blessed Trinity!
In the deep darkness of prayer's stillest night
We worship Thee blinded with light.
Holy Trinity!
Blessed Equal Three,
One God, we praise Thee.

O Blessed Trinity!
Oh would that we could die of love for Thee,
Incomparable Trinity!
Holy Trinity!
Blessed Equal Three,
One God, we praise Thee.

—*Frederick William Faber, 1814-1863*

MAJESTY DIVINE!

Full of glory, full of wonders,
Majesty Divine!
Mid Thine everlasting thunders
How Thy lightnings shine!
Shoreless Ocean! who shall sound Thee?
Thine own eternity is round Thee,
Majesty Divine!

Timeless, spaceless, single, lonely,
Yet sublimely Three,
Thou art grandly, always, only
God in Unity!
Lone in grandeur, lone in glory,
Who shall tell Thy wondrous story,
Awful Trinity?

Speechlessly, without beginning,
Sun that never rose!
Vast, adorable, and winning,
Day that hath no close!
Bliss from Thine own glory tasting,
Everliving, everlasting,
Life that never grows!

Thine own Self for ever filling
With self-kindled flame,
In Thyself Thou art distilling
Unctions without name!
Without worshipping of creatures
Without veiling of Thy features,
God always the same!

In Thy praise of Self untiring
Thy perfections shine;
Self-sufficient, self-admiring,—
Such life must be Thine;—
Glorifying Self, yet blameless
With a sanctity all shameless
It is so divine!

Mid Thine uncreated morning,
Like a trembling star
I behold creation's dawning
Glimmering from afar;
Nothing giving, nothing taking,
Nothing changing, nothing breaking,
Waiting at time's bar!

I with life and love diurnal
See myself in Thee,
All embalmed in love eternal,
Floating in Thy sea:
'Mid Thine uncreated whiteness
I behold Thy glory's brightness
Feed itself on me.

Splendours upon splendours beaming
Change and intertwine;
Glories over glories streaming
All translucent shine!
Blessings, praises adorations
Greet Thee from the trembling nations
Majesty Divine!

—Frederick William Faber, 1814-1863

THE VISION OF THE GODHEAD

Unchanging and Unchangeable, before angelic eyes,
The Vision of the Godhead in its tranquil beauty lies;
And, like a city lighted up all gloriously within,
Its countless lustres glance and gleam, and sweetest worship win.
On the Unbegotten Father, awful well-spring of the Three,
On the Sole Begotten Son's coequal Majesty.
On Him eternally breathed forth from Father and from Son.
The spirits gaze with fixed amaze, and unreckoned ages run.

> Chorus:
> Myriad, myriad angels raise
> Happy hymns of wondering praise,
> Ever through eternal days,
> Before the Holy Trinity,
> One Undivided Three!

Still the Fountain of the Godhead give the forth eternal being:
Still begetting, unbegotten, still His own perfection seeing,
Still limiting His own loved Self with His dear coequal Spirit,
No change comes o'er that blissful Life, no shadow passeth near it.
And beautiful dread Attributes, all manifold and bright,
Now thousands seem, now lose themselves in one self-living light;
And far in that deep Life of God, in harmony complete,
Like crowned kings, all opposite perfections take their seat
And in that ungrowing vision nothing deepens, nothing brightens,
But the living Life of God perpetually lightens;
And created life is nothing but a radiant shadow fleeing
From the unapproached lustres of that Unbeginning Being;

Spirits wise and deep have watched that everlasting Ocean,
And never o'er its lucid field hath rippled faintest motion;
In glory undistinguished never have the Three seemed One,
Nor ever in divided streams the Single Essence run.

There reigns the Eternal Father, in His lone prerogatives,
And, in the Father's Mind, the Son, all self-existing, lives,
With Him, their mutual Jubilee, that deepest depth of love,
Lifegiving Life of two-fold source, the many gifted Dove!
O Bountiful! O Beautiful! can Power or Wisdom add
Fresh features to a life, so munificent and glad?
Can even uncreated Love, ye angels! give a hue
Which can ever make the Unchanging and Unchangeable look new?

The Mercy of the Merciful is equal to Their Might,
As wondrous as Their Love, and as Their Wisdom bright!
As They, who out of nothing called creation at the first,
In everlasting purposes Their own design had nursed,—
As They, who in their solitude, Three Persons, once abode,
Vouchsafed of Their abundance to become creation's God,—
What They owed not to Themselves They stooped to owe to man,
And pledged Their glory to him, in an unimaginable plan.

See! deep within the glowing depth of that Eternal Light.
What change hath come, what vision new transports angelic sight?
A creature can it be, in uncreated bliss?
A novelty in God? Oh what nameless thing is this?
The beauty of the Father's Power is o'er it brightly shed,
The sweetness of the Spirit's Love is unction on its head;
In the wisdom of the Son it plays its wondrous part,
While it lives the loving life of a real Human heart!

A Heart that hath a Mother, and a treasure of red blood,
A Heart that man can pray to, and feed upon for food!
In the brightness of the Godhead is its marvellous abode,
A change in the Unchanging, creation touching God!
Ye spirits blest, in endless rest, who on that Vision gaze,
Salute the Sacred Heart with all your worshipful amaze,
And adore, while with ecstatic skill the Three in One ye scan,
The Mercy that hath planted there that blessed Heart of Man!

All tranquilly, all tranquilly, doth that Blissful Vision last,
And Its brightness o'er immortalized creation will it cast;
Ungrowing and unfading, Its pure Essence doth it keep,
In the deepest of those depths where all are infinitely deep;
Unchanging and Unchangeable as It hath ever been,
As It was before that Human heart was there by angels seen,
So is it at this very hour, so will it ever be,
With that Human Heart within It, beating hot with love of me!

Chorus:

Myriad, myriad angels raise
Happy hymns of wondering praise,
Ever through eternal days,
Before the Holy Trinity,
One Undivided Three!

—Frederick William Faber, 1814-1863

THE THOUGHT OF GOD

The thought of God, the thought of Thee,
Who liest in my heart,
And yet beyond imagined space
Outstretched and present art,—

The thought of Thee, above, below,
Around me and within,
Is more to me than health and wealth,
Or love of kith and kin.

The thought of God is like the tree
Beneath whose shade I lie,
And watch the fleets of snowy clouds
Sail o'er the silent sky.

'Tis like that soft invading light,
Which in all darkness shines,
The thread that through life's sombre web
In golden pattern twines.

It is a thought which ever makes
Life's sweetest smiles from tears,
And is a daybreak to our hopes,
A sunset to our fears;

One while it bids the tears to flow,
Then wipes them from the eyes,
Most often fills our souls with joy,
And always sanctifies.

Within a thought so great, our souls
Little and modest grow,
And, by its vastness awed, we learn
The art of walking slow.

The wild flower on the mossy ground
Scarce bends its pliant form,
When overhead the autumnal wood
Is thundering like a storm.

So is it with our humbled souls
Down in the thought of God,
Scarce conscious in their sober peace
Of the wild storms abroad.

To think of Thee is almost prayer,
And is outspoken praise;
And pain can even passive thoughts
To actual worship raise.

O Lord! I live always in pain,
My life's sad undersong,
Pain in itself not hard to bear,
But hard to bear so long.

Little sometimes weighs more than much,
When it has no relief;
A joyless life is worse to bear
Than one of active grief.

And yet, O Lord! a suffering life
One grand ascent may dare;
Penance, not self-imposed, can make
The whole of life a prayer.

All murmurs he inside Thy Will
Which are to Thee addressed;
To suffer for Thee is our work,
To think of Thee our rest.

—*Frederick William Faber, 1814-1863*

THE GREATNESS OF GOD

O Majesty unspeakable and dread!
Wert Thou less mighty than Thou art,
Thou wert, O Lord! too great for our belief,
Too little for our heart.

Thy greatness would seem monstrous by the side
Of creatures frail and undivine;
Yet they would have a greatness of their own
Free and apart from Thine.

Such grandeur were but a created thing,
A spectre, terror, and a grief,
Out of all keeping with a world so calm,
Oppressing our belief.

But greatness, which is infinite makes room
For all things in its lap to lie;
We should be crushed by a magnificence
Short of infinity.

It would outgrow us from the face of things,
Still prospering as we decayed,
And, like a tyrannous rival, it would feed
Upon the wrecks it made.

But what is infinite must be a home,
A shelter for the meanest fife,
Where it is free to reach its greatest growth
Far from the touch of strife.

We share in what is infinite: 'tis ours,
For we and it alike are Thine;
What I enjoy, great God! by right of Thee
Is more than doubly mine.

Thus doth Thy hospitable greatness lie
Outside us like a boundless sea;
We cannot lose ourselves where all is home,
Nor drift away from Thee.

Out on that sea we are in harbour still,
And scarce advert to winds and tides,
Like ships that ride at anchor, with the waves
Flapping against their sides.

Thus doth Thy grandeur make us grand ourselves;
'Tis goodness bids us fear;
Thy greatness makes us brave as children are,
When those they love are near.

Great God, our lowliness takes heart to play
Beneath the shadow of Thy state;
The only comfort of our littleness
Is that Thou art so great.

Then on Thy grandeur I will lay me down;
Already life is heaven for me;
No cradled child more softly lies than I,—
Come soon, Eternity!

—Frederick William Faber, 1814-1863

THE ETERNITY OF GOD

O Lord! my heart is sick,
Sick of this everlasting change;
And life runs tediously quick
Through its unresting race and varied range:
Change finds no likeness to itself in Thee,
And wakes no echo in Thy mute Eternity.

Dear Lord! my heart is sick
Of this perpetual lapsing time,
So slow in grief, in joy so quick,
Yet ever casting shadows so sublime;
Time of all creatures is least like to Thee,
And yet it is our share of Thine eternity.

O change and time are storms
For lives so thin and frail as ours;
For change the work of grace deforms
With love that soils, and help that overpowers;
And time is strong, and, like some chafing sea,
It seems to fret the shores of Thine eternity.

Weak, weak, forever weak!
We cannot hold what we possess;
Youth cannot find, age will not seek,
O weakness is the heart's worst weariness:
But weakest hearts can lift their thoughts to Thee;
It makes us strong to think of Thine eternity.

Thou hadst no youth, great God,
An Unbeginning End Thou art;
Thy glory in itself abode,
And still abides in its own tranquil heart:
No age can heap its outward years on Thee:
Dear God! Thou art Thyself Thine own eternity!

Without an end or bound
Thy life lies all outspread in light;
Our lives feel Thy life all around,
Making our weakness strong, our darkness bright;
Yet is it neither wilderness nor sea,
But the calm gladness of a full eternity.

Oh Thou art very great
To set Thyself so far above!
But we partake of Thine estate,
Established in Thy strength and in Thy love:
That love hath made eternal room for me
In the sweet vastness of its own eternity.

Oh Thou art very meek
To overshade Thy creatures thus!
Thy grandeur is the shade we seek:
To be eternal is Thy use to us:
Ah Blessed God! what joy it is to me
To lose all thought of self in Thine eternity.

Self-wearied, Lord! I come;
For I have lived my life too fast:
Now that years bring me nearer home
Grace must be slowly used to make it last;
When my heart beats too quick I think of Thee,
And of the leisure of Thy long eternity.

Farewell, vain joys of earth!
Farewell, all love that is not His!
Dear God! be Thou my only mirth,
Thy majesty my single timid bliss!
Oh in the bosom of eternity
Thou does not weary of Thyself, nor we of Thee!

—Frederick William Faber, 1814-1863

THE FEAR OF GOD

My fear of Thee, O Lord, exults
Like life within my veins,
A fear which rightly claims to be
One of love's sacred pains.

Thy goodness to Thy saints of old
An awful thing appeared;
For were Thy majesty less good
Much less would it be feared.

There is no joy the soul can meet
Upon life's various road
Like the sweet fear that sits and shrinks
Under the eye of God.

A special joy is in all love
For objects we revere;
Thus joy in God will always be
Proportioned to our fear.

Oh Thou art greatly to be feared,
Thou art so prompt to bless!
The dread to miss such love as Thine
Makes fear but love's excess.

The fulness of Thy mercy seems
To fill both land and sea;
If we can break through bounds so vast,
How exiled shall we be!

For grace is fearful, which each hour
Our path in life has crossed;
If it were rarer, it might be
Less easy to be lost.

But fear is love, and love is fear,
And in and out they move;
But fear is an intenser joy
Than mere unfrightened love.

When most I fear Thee, Lord! then most
Familiar I appear;
And I am in my soul most free,
When I am most in fear.

I should not love Thee as I do,
If love might make more free;
Its very sweetness would be lost
In greater liberty.

I feel Thee most a father, when
I fancy Thee most near:
And Thou comest not so nigh in love
As Thou comest, Lord! in fear.

They love Thee little, if at all,
Who do not fear Thee much;
If love is Thine attraction, Lord!
Fear is Thy very touch.

Love could not love Thee half so much
If it found Thee not so near;
It is thy nearness, which makes love
The perfectness of fear.

We fear because Thou art so good,
And because we can sin;
And when we make most show of love,
We are trembling most within.

And Father! when to us in heaven
Thou shalt Thy Face unveil,
Then more than ever will our souls
Before Thy goodness quail.

Our blessedness will be to bear
The sight of Thee so near,
And thus eternal love will be
But the ecstasy of fear.

—Frederick William Faber, 1814-1863

THE ETERNAL FATHER

Father! the sweetest, dearest Name.
That men or angels know!
Fountain of life, that had no fount
From which itself could flow!

Thy life is one unwearing day;
Before its Now Thou hast
No varied future yet unlived,
No lapse of changeless past.

Thou comest not, Thou goest not;
Thou wert not, wilt not be;
Eternity is but a thought
By which we think of Thee.

No epochs lie behind Thy life;
Thou holdst Thy life of none:
No other life is by Thy side;
Thine is supremely lone.

Far upward in the timeless past,
Ere form or space had come,
We see Thee by Thine own dread light,
Thyself Thine only home.

Thy vastness is not young or old;
Thy life hath never grown;
No time can measure out Thy days.
No space can make Thy throne.

Thy life is deep within Thyself,
Sole Unbegotten Sire!
But Son and Spirit flow from Thee
In coeternal fire.

They flow from Thee, They rest in Thee,
As in a Father's Breast-
Processions of eternal love,
Pulses of eternal rest!

That They in majesty should reign
Coequal, Sire! with Thee,
But magnifies the singleness
Of Thy paternity.

Their uncreated glories, Lord!
With Thine own glory shine;
Thy glory as the Father needs
That Theirs should equal Thine.

All things are equal in Thy life:
Thou joyst to be alone,
To have no sire, and yet to have
A coeternal Son.

Thy Spirit is Thy jubilee;
Thy Word is Thy delight;
Thou givest Them to equal Thee
In glory and in might.

Thou art too great to keep unshared
Thy grand eternity;
They have it as Thy gift to Them,
Which is no gift to Thee.

We too, like Thy coequal Word,
Within Thy lap may rest:
We too, like Thine Eternal Dove,
May nestle in Thy Breast.

Lone Fountain of the Godhead! hail!
Person most dread and dear!
I thrill with frightened joy to feel
Thy fatherhood so near.

Lost in Thy greatness, Lord! I live,
As in some gorgeous maze;
Thy sea of unbegotten light
Blinds me, and yet I gaze.

For Thy grandeur is all tenderness,
All motherlike and meek;
The hearts that will not come to it
Humbling itself to seek.

Thou feign'st to be remote, and speakst
As if from far above,
That fear may make more bold with Thee
And be beguiled to love.

On earth Thou hidest, not to scare
The children with Thy light,
Then showest us Thy Face in heaven,
When we can bear the sight.

All fathers learn their craft from Thee;
All loves are shadows cast
From the beautiful eternal hills
Of Thine unbeginning past.

—*Frederick William Faber, 1814-1863*

THE ETERNAL GENERATION OF THE SON

Amid the eternal silences
God's endless Word was spoken;
None heard but He who always spake,
And the silence was unbroken.

                Chorus.

Oh marvellous! Oh worshipful!
No song or sound is heard,
But everywhere and every hour,
In love, in wisdom, and in power,
The Father speaks His dear Eternal Word.

For ever in the eternal land
The glorious day is dawning;
For ever is the Father's Light
Like an endless outspread morning.

From the Father's vast tranquillity,
In light coequal glowing
The kingly consubstantial Word
Is unutterably flowing.

For ever climbs that Morning Star
Without ascent or motion;
For ever is its daybreak shed
On the Spirit's boundless ocean.

O Word! who fitly can adore
Thy Birth and Thy Relation,
Lost in the impenetrable light
Of Thine awful Generation?

Thy Father clasps Thee evermore
In unspeakable embraces,
While angels tremble as they praise,
And shroud their dazzled faces.

And oh! in what abyss of love,
So fiery yet so tender,
The Holy Ghost encircles Thee
With His uncreated splendour!

O Word! O dear and gentle Word!
Thy creatures kneel before Thee,
And in ecstacies of timid love
Delightedly adore Thee.

Hail choicest mystery of God!
Hail wondrous Generation!
The Father's self-sufficient rest!
The Spirit's jubilation!

Dear Person! dear beyond all words,
Glorious beyond all telling!
Oh with what songs of silent love
Our ravished hearts are swelling!

      Chorus.

O! marvellous! O worshipful!
No song or sound is heard,
But everywhere and every hour,
In love, in wisdom, and in power,
The Father speaks His dear Eternal Word.
   —*FREDERICK WILLIAM FABER, 1814-1863*

THE HOLY SPIRIT

Fountain of Love! Thyself true God!
Who through eternal days
From Father and from Son hast flowed
In uncreated ways!

O Majesty unspeakable!
O Person all divine!
How in the Threefold Majesty
Doth Thy Procession shine!

Fixed in the Godhead's awful light
Thy fiery Breath doth move;
Thou art a wonder by Thyself
To worship and to love!

Proceeding, yet of equal age
With those whose love Thou art:
Proceeding, yet distinct, from those
From whom Thou seem'st to part.

And undivided Nature shared
With Father and with Son;
A Person by Thyself; with Them
Thy simple essence One;

Bond art Thou of the other Twain!
Omnipotent and free!
The consummating Love of God!
The Limit of the Three!

Thou limitest infinity,
Thyself all infinite;
The Godhead lives, and loves, and rests,
In Thine eternal light.

I dread Thee, Unbegotten Love!
True God! sole Fount of Grace!
And now before Thy Blessed throne
My sinful self abase.

Ocean, wide-flowing Ocean, Thou,
Of uncreated Love;
I tremble as within my soul
I feel Thy waters move.

Thou art a sea without a shore;
Awful, immense Thou art;
A sea which can contract itself
Within my narrow heart.

And yet Thou art a haven too
Out on the shoreless sea,
A harbor that can hold full well
Shipwrecked Humanity.

Thou art an unborn Breath outbreathed
On angels and on men,
Subduing all things to Thyself,
We know not how or when.

Thou art a God of fire, that doth
Create while He consumes!
A God of light, whose rays on earth
Darken where He illumes!

All things! dread Spirit! to Thy praise
Thy Presence doth transmute;
Evil itself Thy glory bears,
Its one abiding fruit!

O Light! O Love! O very God
I dare no longer gaze
Upon Thy wondrous attributes,
And their mysterious ways.

O Spirit, beautiful and dread!
My heart is fit to break
With love of all Thy tenderness
For us poor sinners' sake.

Thy love of Jesus I adore;
My comfort this shall be,
That, when I serve my dearest Lord,
That service worships Thee!

—FREDERICK WILLIAM FABER, 1814-1863

PENTECOST

He comes! He comes! that mighty Breath
From heaven's eternal shores;
His uncreated freshness fills
His bride as she adores.

Earth quakes before that rushing blast,
Heaven echoes back the sound,
And mightily the tempest wheels
That Upper Room around.

One moment—and the silentness
Was breathless as the grave;
The fluttered earth forgot to quake,
The troubled trees to wave.

One moment—and the Spirit hung
O'er them with dread desire;
Then broke upon the heads of all
In cloven tongues of fire.

What gifts He gave those chosen men
Past ages can display;
Nay more, their vigour still inspires
The weakness of today.

Those tongues still speak within the Church,
That Fire is undecayed;
Its well-spring was that Upper Room,
Where the disciples met and prayed.

The Spirit came into the Church
With His unfailing power;
He is the Living Heart that beats
Within her at this hour.

Speak gently then of Church and Saints,
Lest you His ways reprove;
The Heat, the Pulses of the Church
Are God's Eternal Love.

Oh let us fall and worship Him,
The Love of Sire and Son,
The Consubstantial Breath of God,
The Coeternal One!

Ah! see, how like the Incarnate Word,
His Blessed Self He lowers,
To dwell with us invisibly,
And make His riches ours.

Most tender Spirit! Mighty God!
Sweet must Thy Presence be,
If loss of Jesus can be gain,
So long as we have Thee!

—FREDERICK WILLIAM FABER, 1814-1863

Devotional Meditations on the Cross of Christ

IF SWEET THE MOMENTS, RICH IN BLESSING

Sweet the moments, rich in blessing,
Which before the Cross I spend;
Life and health and peace possessing
From the sinner's dying Friend.

Truly blessed is this station,
Low before His Cross to lie;
While I see divine compassion
Beaming in His languid eye.

Love and grief my heart dividing,
With my tears His feet I'll bathe;
Constant still in faith abiding,
Life deriving from His death.

For Thy sorrows we adore Thee—
For the griefs that wrought our peace—
Gracious Saviour! we implore Thee,
In our hearts Thy love increase.

—*WALTER SHIRLEY et al., 1725-1786*

RIDE ON! RIDE ON IN MAJESTY!

Ride on! ride on in majesty!
Ride on! ride on in majesty!
Hark! all the tribes "Hosanna" cry:
O Saviour meek, pursue Thy road
With palms and scattered garments strowed.

Ride on! ride on in majesty!
In lowly pomp ride on to die:
O Christ, Thy triumphs now begin
O'er captive death and conquered sin.

Ride on! ride on in majesty!
The winged squadrons of the sky
Look down with sad and wondering eyes
To see the approaching sacrifice.

Ride on! Ride on in majesty!
Thy last and fiercest strife is nigh;
The Father on His sapphire throne
Awaits His own anointed Son.

Ride on! ride on in majesty!
In lowly pomp ride on to die;
Bow Thy meek head to mortal pain,
Then take, O God, Thy power and reign.

—HENRY HART MILMAN, 1791-1868

WOULD JESUS HAVE THE SINNER DIE?

Would Jesus have the sinner die?
Why hangs He then on yonder tree?
What means that strange expiring cry?
(Sinners, He prays for you and me;)
Forgive them, Father, O forgive!
They know not that by Me they live.

Jesus, descended from above,
Our loss of Eden to retrieve,
Great God of universal love,
If all the world through Thee may live,
In us a quick'ning spirit be,
And witness Thou hast died for me.

Thou loving, all-atoning Lamb, —
Thee, by Thy painful agony,
Thy bloody sweat, Thy grief and shame,
Thy cross and passion on the tree,
Thy precious death and life—I pray,
Take all, take all my sins away.

O let Thy love my heart constrain, —
Thy love, for every sinner free, —
That every fallen son of man
May taste the grace that found out me;
That all mankind with me may prove
Thy sov'reign, everlasting love.

—*CHARLES WESLEY, 1707-1767*

HE DIES! THE FRIEND OF SINNERS DIES!

He dies! the Friend of sinners dies!
Lo! Salem's daughters weep around;
A solemn darkness veils the skies,
A sudden trembling shakes the ground:
Come, saints, and drop a tear or two
For Him who groan'd beneath your load;
He shed a thousand drops for you, —
A thousand drops of richer blood.

Here's love and grief beyond degree:
The Lord of glory dies for man!
But lo! what sudden joys we see:
Jesus, the dead, revives again.
The rising God forsakes the tomb;
(In vain the tomb forbids His rise;)
Cherubic legions guard Him home,
And shout Him welcome to the skies.

Break off your tears, ye saints, and tell
How high your great Deliv'rer reigns;
Sing how He spoil'd the hosts of hell,
And led the monster death in chains:
Say, Live forever, wondrous King!
Born to redeem, and strong to save;
Then ask the monster, Where's thy sting?
And, Where's thy vict'ry, boasting grave?

—ISAAC WATRS, 1674-1748

BEFORE THE CROSS

My Lord, my Master, at Thy feet adoring,
I see Thee bowed beneath Thy load of woe:
For me, a sinner, is Thy life-blood pouring;
For Thee, my Saviour, scarce my tears will flow.

Thine own disciple to the Jews has sold Thee,
With friendship's kiss and loyal word he came;
How oft of faithful love my lips have told Thee,
While Thou hast seen my falsehood and my shame!

With taunts and scoffs they mock what seems Thy weakness,
With blows and outrage adding pain to pain;
Thou art unmoved and steadfast in Thy meekness;
When I am wronged how quickly I complain!

My Lord, my Saviour, when I see Thee wearing
Upon Thy bleeding brow the crown of thorn,
Shall I for pleasure live, or shrink from bearing
Whate'er my lot may be of pain or scorn?

O Victim of Thy love, O pangs most healing,
O saving death, O wounds that I adore,
O shame most glorious! Christ, before Thee kneeling,
I pray Thee keep me Thine for evermore.

—From the French of JACQUES BRIDAINE, 1701-1767
Tr. THOMAS BENSON POLLOCK, 1836-1896

O SACRED HEAD, NOW WOUNDED

O Sacred Head, now wounded,
With grief and shame weighed down,
Now scornfully surrounded
With thorns, Thine only crown;
O sacred Head, what glory,
What bliss, till now was Thine!
Yet though despised and gory,
I joy to call Thee mine.

What Thou, my Lord, hast suffered
Was all for sinners' gain;
Mine, mine was the transgression,
But Thine the deadly pain;
Lo, here I fall, my Saviour!
'Tis I deserve Thy place;
Look on me with Thy favor,
Vouchsafe to me Thy grace.

What language shall I borrow
To thank Thee, dearest Friend,
For this Thy dying sorrow,
Thy pity without end?
Oh, make me Thine forever;
And should I fainting be,
Lord, let me never, never
Outlive my love to Thee!

Be near me when I'm dying;
Oh, show Thy Cross to me!
And for my succor flying;
Come, Lord, and set me free!
These eyes, new faith receiving,
From Jesus shall not move;
For he who dies believing,
Dies safely, through Thy love.

—*BERNARD OF CLAIRVAUX, 1091-1153*
Tr. PAUL GERHARDT, 1607-1676
English tr., JAMES WADDELL ALEXANDER, 1859-1904

NOT ALL THE BLOOD OF BEASTS

Not all the blood of beasts,
On Jewish altars slain,
Could give the guilty conscience peace,
Or wash away the stain.

But Christ, the heavenly Lamb,
Takes all our sins away;

A sacrifice of nobler name,
And richer blood than they.

My faith would lay her hand
On that dear head of Thine,
While like a penitent I stand,
And there confess my sin.

My soul looks back, to see
The burdens Thou didst bear,
When hanging on the cursed tree,
And hopes her guilt was there.

Believing, we rejoice
To see the curse remove;
We bless the Lamb with cheerful voice,
And sing His bleeding love.

—ISAAC WATTS, 1674-1748

PENITENTIAL REFLECTIONS ON OUR SINS

MY SINS, MY SAVIOUR!

My sins, my sins, my Saviour!
They take such hold on me,
I am not able to look up,
Save only Christ to Thee;
In Thee is all forgiveness,
In Thee abundant grace,
My shadow and my sunshine
The brightness of Thy face.

My sins, my sins, my Saviour!
How sad on Thee they fall;
Seen through Thy gentle patience,
I ten-fold feel them all;
I know they are forgiven,
But still, their pain to me
Is all the grief and anguish
They laid, my Lord, on Thee.

My sins, my sins, my Saviour!
Their guilt I never knew
Till with Thee in the desert
I near Thy passion drew;
Till with Thee in the garden
I heard Thy pleading pray'r,
And saw the sweat-drops bloody
That told Thy sorrow there.

Therefore my songs, my Saviour,
E'en in this time of woe,
Shall tell of all Thy goodness
To suffering man below;
Thy goodness and Thy favor,
Whose presence from above
Rejoice those hearts my Saviour,
That live in Thee alone.

—*JOHN S. B. MONSELL, 1811-1875*

HAVE MERCY, GOD MOST HIGH

Have mercy on us, God Most High!
Who lift our hearts to Thee;
Have mercy on us worms of earth,
Most holy Trinity!

Most ancient of all mysteries!
Before Thy throne we lie;
Have mercy now most merciful,
Most holy Trinity!

When heaven and earth were yet unmade,
When time was yet unknown,
Thou in Thy bliss and majesty
Didst live and love alone!

Thou wert not born; there was no fount
From which Thy Being flowed;
There is no end which Thou canst reach:
But Thou art simply God.

How wonderful creation is,
The work that Thou didst bless,
And, oh! what then must Thou be like,
Eternal Loveliness?

How beautiful the Angels are,
The Saints how bright in bliss;
But with Thy beauty, Lord! compared,
How dull, how poor is this!

No wonder Saints have died of love,
No wonder hearts can break,
Pure hearts that once have learned to love
God for His own dear sake.

O listen, then, Most Pitiful!
To Thy poor creature's heart;
It blesses Thee that Thou art God,
That Thou art what Thou art!

Most ancient of all mysteries!
Still at Thy throne we lie;
Have mercy now, most merciful,
Most holy Trinity!

—FREDERICK WILLIAM FABER, 1814-1863

O LORD, I AM ASHAMED TO SEEK THY FACE

O Lord, I am ashamed to seek Thy Face
As tho' I loved Thee as Thy saints love Thee:
Yet turn from those Thy lovers, look on me,
Disgrace me not with uttermost disgrace;
But pour on me ungracious, pour Thy grace
To purge my heart and bid my will go free,
Till I too taste Thy hidden Sweetness, see
Thy hidden Beauty in the holy place.
O Thou Who callest sinners to repent,
Call me Thy sinner unto penitence,
For many sins grant me the greater love:
Set me above the waterfloods, above
Devil and shifting world and fleshly sense,
Thy Mercy's all-amazing monument.

—CHRISTINA ROSSETTI, 1830-1894

SCOURGE, BUT RECEIVE ME

Good Lord, today
I scarce find breath to say:
Scourge, but receive me.
For stripes are hard to bear, but worse
Thy intolerable curse;
So do not leave me.

Good Lord, lean down
In pity, tho' Thou frown;
Smite, but retrieve me:
For so Thou hold me up to stand
And kiss Thy smiting hand,
It less will grieve me.

—*CHRISTINA ROSSETTI, 1830-1894*

Rejoicing in Forgiveness and Justification

SONG OF ASSURANCE

Now I have found the ground wherein
Sure my soul's anchor may remain,
The wounds of Jesus, for my sin
Before the world's foundation slain;
Whose mercy shall unshaken stay,
When heaven and earth are fled away.

Father, Thine everlasting grace
Our scanty thought surpasses far:
Thy heart still melts with tenderness.
Thy arms of love still open are,
Returning sinners to receive,
That mercy they may taste and live.

O Love, Thou bottomless abyss,
My sins are swallowed up in Thee!
Covered is my unrighteousness,
Nor spot of guilt remains on me,
While Jesus' blood, through earth and skies,
Mercy, free, boundless mercy, cries.

With faith I plunge me in this sea;
Here is my hope, my joy, my rest;
Hither, when hell assails, I flee,
I look into my Saviour's breast;
Away, sad doubt, and anxious fear!
Mercy is all that's written there.

Though waves and storms go o'er my head,
Though strength, and health, and friends be gone,
Though joys be withered all and dead,
Though every comfort be withdrawn,
On this my steadfast soul relies, —
Father, Thy mercy never dies.

Fixed on this ground will I remain,
Though my heart fail, and flesh decay;
This anchor shall my soul sustain,
When earth's foundations melt away;
Mercy's full power I then shall prove,
Loved with an everlasting love.

—*JOHANN ANDREAS ROTHE, 1688-1758*
Tr. JOHN WESLEY, 1703-1791

A GOOD CONFESSION

The chains that have bound me are flung to the wind,
By the mercy of God the poor slave is set free;
And the strong grace of heaven breathes fresh o'er the mind,
Like the bright winds of summer that gladden the sea.

There was nought in God's world half so dark or so vile
As the sin and the bondage that fettered my soul;
There was nought half so base as the malice and guile
Of my own sordid passions, or Satan's control.

For years I have borne about hell in my breast;
When I thought of my God it was nothing but gloom;
Day brought me no pleasure, night gave me no rest,
There was still the grim shadow of horrible doom.

It seemed as if nothing less likely could be
Than that light should break in on a dungeon so deep;
To create a new world were less hard than to free
The slave from his bondage, the soul from its sleep.

But the word had gone forth, and said, Let there be light,
And it flashed through my soul like a sharp passing smart;
One look to my Saviour, and all the dark night,
Like a dream scarce remembered, was gone from my heart.

I cried out for mercy, and fell on my knees,
And confessed, while my heart with keen sorrow was wrung;
'Twas the labor of minutes, and years of disease
Fell as fast from my soul as the words from my tongue.

And now, blest be God and the sweet Lord who died!
No deer on the mountain, no bird in the sky
No bright wave that leaps on the dark bounding tide,
Is a creature so free or so happy as I.

All hail, then, all hail, to the dear Precious Blood,
That hath worked these sweet wonders of mercy in me;
May each day countless numbers throng down to its flood,
And God have His glory, and sinners go free.

—FREDERICK WILLIAM FABER, 1814-1863

A SOUL IN ITS EARLIEST LOVE

O how happy are they
Who their Saviour obey,
And have laid up their treasure above;
Tongue can never express
The sweet comfort and peace
Of a soul in its earliest love.

That sweet comfort was mine,
When the favor divine
I received through the blood of the Lamb;
When my heart first believed,
What a joy I received—
What a heaven in Jesus' Name!

'Twas a heaven below
My Redeemer to know,
And the angels could do nothing more
Than to fall at His feet,
And the story repeat,
And the Lover of sinners adore.

Jesus all the day long
Was my joy and my song:
O that all His salvation might see;
He hath loved me, I cried,
He hath suffered and died,
To redeem even rebels like me.

O the rapturous height
Of that holy delight
Which I felt in the life-giving blood;
Of my Saviour possessed,
I was perfectly blessed
As if filled with the fulness of God.

—*CHARLES WESLEY, 1707-1788*

Yearning for Purity of Heart

I THIRST, THOU WOUNDED LAMB OF GOD

I thirst, Thou wounded Lamb of God,
To wash me in Thy cleansing blood;
To dwell within Thy wounds; then pain
Is sweet, and life or death is gain.

Take my poor heart, and let it be
Forever closed to all but Thee:
Seal Thou my breast, and let me wear
That pledge of love forever there.

How blest are they who still abide
Close shelter'd in Thy bleeding side!
Who thence their life and strength derive,
And by Thee move, and in Thee live.

What are our works but sin and death,
Till Thou thy quick'ning Spirit breathe?
Thou giv'st the power thy grace to move;
O wondrous grace! O boundless love!

How can it be, Thou heavenly King,
That Thou shouldst us to glory bring;
Make slaves the partners of thy throne,
Deck'd with a never-fading crown?

Hence our hearts melt, our eyes o'erflow,
Our words are lost, nor will we know,
Nor will we think of aught beside, —
My Lord, my Love is crucified.

—Attributed to JOHN WESLEY, 1703-1791

PRAYER FOR PURITY

O Thou, to whose all-searching sight
The darkness shineth as the light,
Search, prove my heart; it pants for Thee;
O burst these bonds, and set it free!

Wash out its stains, refine its dross,
Nail my affections to the Cross;
Hallow each thought; let all within
Be clean, as Thou, my Lord, art clean!

If in this darksome wild I stray,
Be Thou my Light, be Thou my Way;
No foes, no violence I fear,
No fraud, while Thou, my God, art near.

When rising floods my soul o'erflow,
When sinks my heart in waves of woe,
Jesus, Thy timely aid impart,
And raise my head, and cheer my heart.

Saviour, where'er Thy steps I see,
Dauntless, untired, I follow Thee;
O let Thy hand support me still,
And lead me to Thy holy hill!

If rough and thorny be the way,
My strength proportion to my day;
Till toil, and grief, and pain shall cease,
Where all is calm, and joy, and peace.

—*NICOLAUS LUDWIG VON ZINZENDORF, 1700-1760*
Tr. JOHN WESLEY, 1703-1791

JESUS, THINE ALL-VICTORIOUS LOVE

Jesus, thine all-victorious love
Shed in my heart abroad:
Then shall my feet no longer rove,
Rooted and fix'd in God.

O that in me the sacred fire
Might now begin to glow;
Burn up the dross of base desire,
And make the mountains flow.

O that it now from heaven might fall,
And all my sins consume:
Come, Holy Ghost, for Thee I call;
Spirit of burning, come.

Refining fire, go through my heart;
Illuminate my soul;
Scatter Thy life through every part,
And sanctify the whole.

My steadfast soul, from falling free,
Shall then no longer move;
While Christ is all the world to me,
And all my heart is love.

—*CHARLES WESLEY, 1707-1788*

SELF-LOVE

Oh I could go through all life's troubles singing,
Turning earth's night to day,
If self were not so fast around me, clinging
To all I do or say.

My very thoughts are selfish, always building
Mean castles in the air;
I use my love of others for a gilding
To make myself look fair.

I fancy all the world engrossed with judging
My merit or my blame;
Its warmest praise seems an ungracious grudging
Of praise which I might claim.

In youth or age, by city, wood, or mountain,
Self is forgotten never;
Where'er we tread, it gushes like a fountain,
And its waters flow for ever.

Alas! no speed in life can snatch us wholly
Out of self's hateful sight;
And it keeps step, whene'er we travel slowly,
And sleeps with us at night.

No grief's sharp knife, no pain's most cruel sawing
Self and the soul can sever:
The surface, that in joy sometimes seems thawing,
Soon freezes worse than ever.

Thus we are never men, self's wretched swathing
Not letting virtue swell;
Thus is our whole life numbed, for ever bathing
Within this frozen well.

O miserable omnipresence, stretching
Over all time and space,
How have I run from thee, yet found thee reaching
The goal in every race.

Inevitable self! vile imitation
Of universal light, —
Within our hearts a dreadful usurpation
Of God's exclusive right!

The opiate balms of grace may haply still thee,
Deep in my nature lying;
For I may hardly hope, alas! to kill thee,
Save by the act of dying.

O Lord! that I could waste my life for others,
With no ends of my own,
That I could pour myself into my brothers,
And live for them alone!

Such was the life Thou livedst; self-abjuring,
Thine own pains never easing,
Our burdens bearing, our just doom enduring,
A life without self-pleasing!

—FREDERICK WILLIAM FABER, 1814-1863

Aspirations After God

AS PANTS THE HART

As pants the hart for cooling streams,
When heated in the chase;
So longs my soul, O God, for Thee,
And Thy refreshing grace.

For Thee, my God, the living God,
My thirsty soul doth pine;
Oh, when shall I behold Thy face,
Thou Majesty divine?

Why restless, why cast down, my soul?
Trust God; who will employ
His aid for thee, and change these sighs
To thankful hymns of joy.

God of my strength, how long shall I,
Like one forgotten, mourn;
Forlorn, forsaken, and exposed
To my oppressor's scorn?

I sigh to think of happier days,
When Thou, O Lord! wast nigh;
When every heart was tuned to praise,
And none more blessed than I.

Why restless, why cast down, my soul?
Hope still; and thou shalt sing
The praise of Him who is Thy God,
Thy health's eternal spring.

—NAHUM TATE, 1652-1715
—NICHOLAS BRADY, 1659-1726
Psalm 42 paraphrase

THE WAY OF PERFECTION

Oh how the thought of God attracts
And draws the heart from earth,
And sickens it of passing shows
And dissipating mirth!

'Tis not enough to save our souls,
To shun the eternal fires;
The thought of God will rouse the heart
To more sublime desires.

God only is the creature's home,
Though rough and straight the road;
Yet nothing less can satisfy
The love that longs for God.

Oh utter but the Name of God
Down in your heart of hearts,
And see how from the world at once
All tempting light departs.

A trusting heart, a yearning eye,
Can win their way above;
If mountains can be moved by faith,
Is there less power in love?

How little of that road, my soul!
How little hast thou gone!
Take heart, and let the thought of God
Allure thee further on.

The freedom from all wilful sin,
The Christian's daily task, —
Oh these are graces far below
What longing love would ask!

Dole not thy duties out to God,
But let thy hand be free:
Look long at Jesus; His sweet Blood,
How was it dealt to thee?

The perfect way is hard to flesh;
It is not hard to love;
If thou wert sick for want of God,
How swiftly wouldst thou move!

Then keep thy conscience sensitive;
No inward token miss:
And go where grace entices thee; —
Perfection lies in this.

Be docile to thine unseen Guide,
Love Him as He loves thee;
Time and obedience are enough,
And thou a saint shall be.

—*FREDERICK WILLIAM FABER, 1814-1863*

THOU SHEPHERD OF ISRAEL, AND MINE

Thou Shepherd of Israel, and mine,
The joy and desire of my heart,
For closer communion I pine;
I long to reside where Thou art:
The pasture I languish to find,
Where all, who their Shepherd obey,
Are fed, on Thy bosom reclined,
And screen'd from the heat of the day.

'Tis there, with the lambs of Thy flock,
There only, I covet to rest;
To lie at the foot of the rock,
Or rise to be hid in Thy breast:
'Tis there I would always abide,
And never a moment depart, —
Conceal'd in the cleft of Thy side,
Eternally held in Thy heart.

—*CHARLES WESLEY, 1707-1788*

THE FERVOR OF HOLY DESIRE

Still, still, without ceasing,
I feel it increasing,
This fervor of holy desire;
And often exclaim,
Let me die in the flame
Of a love that can never expire!

Had I words to explain,
What she must sustain,
Who dies to the world and its ways;
How joy and affright,
Distress and delight,
Alternately checker her days;

Thou, sweetly severe!
I would make thee appear,
In all thou art pleas'd to award,
Not more in the sweet,
Than the bitter I meet,
My tender and merciful Lord.

This Faith, in the dark
Pursuing its mark,
Through many sharp trials of Love,
Is the sorrowful waste,
That is to be pass'd,
In the way to the Canaan above.

—*JEANNE MARIE DE LA MOTTE-GUYON, 1648-1717*

Tr. Unknown

DESIRE OF GOD

Oh for freedom, for freedom in worshipping God,
For the mountain-top feeling of generous souls,
For the health, for the air, of the hearts deep and broad,
Where grace not in rills but in cataracts rolls!

Most good is the brisk wholesome service of fear,
And the calm wise obedience of conscience is sweet;
And good are all worships, all loyalties dear,
All promptitudes fitting, all services meet.

But none honours God like the thirst of desire,
Nor possesses the heart so completely with Him;
For it burns the world out with the swift ease of fire,
And fills life with good works till it runs o'er the brim.

Then pray for desire, for love's wistfullest yearning,
For the beautiful pining of holy desire;
Yes, pray for a soul that is ceaselessly burning
With the soft fragrant flames of this thrice happy fire.

For the heart only dwells, truly dwells with its treasure,
And the languor of love captive hearts can unfetter;
And they who love God cannot love Him by measure,
For their love is but hunger to love Him still better.

Is it hard to serve God, timid soul? Hast thou found
Gloomy forests, dark glens, mountain-tops on thy way?
All the hard would be easy, all the tangles unwound,
Wouldst thou only desire, as well as obey.

For the lack of desire is the ill of all ills;
Many thousands through it the dark pathway have trod,
The balsam, the wine of predestinate wills
Is a jubilant pining and longing for God.

'Tis a fire that will burn what thou canst not pass over;
'Tis a lightning that breaks away all bars to love;
'Tis a sunbeam the secrets of God to discover;
'Tis the wing David prayed for, the wing of the Dove.

I have seen living men—and their good angels know
How they failed and fell short through the want of desire:
Souls once almost saints have descended so low,
'Twill be much if their wings bear them over the fire.

I have seen dying men not so grand in their dying
As our love would have wished,—and through lack of desire:
Oh that we may die languishing, burning, and sighing;
For God's last grace and best is to die all on fire.

'Tis a great gift of God to live after our Lord,
Yet the old Hebrew times they were ages of fire.
When fainting souls fed on each dim figured word,
And God called men He loved most—the Men of Desire.

Oh then wish more for God, burn more with desire,
Covet more the dear sight of his marvellous Face;
Pray louder, pray longer, for the sweet gift of fire
To come down on thy heart with its whirlwinds of grace.

Yes, pine for thy God, fainting soul! Ever pine;
Oh languish mid all that life brings thee of mirth;
Famished, thirsty, and restless,—let such life be thine,—
For what sight is to heaven, desire is to earth.

God loves to be longed for, He loves to be sought,
For He sought us Himself with such longing and love:
He died for desire of us, marvellous thought!
And He yearns for us now to be with Him above.

—FREDERICK WILLIAM FABER, 1814-1863

SATISFIED

Draw me to Thee, till far within Thy rest,
In stillness of Thy peace, Thy voice I hear—
For ever quieted upon Thy breast,
So loved, so near.

By mystery of Thy touch my spirit thrilled,
O Magnet all Divine;
The hunger of my soul for ever stilled,
For Thou art mine.

For me, O Lord, the world is all too small,
For I have seen Thy face,
Where Thine eternal love irradiates all
Within Thy secret place.
And therefore from all others, from all else,
Draw Thou my soul to Thee . . .
. . . Yea—Thou hast broken the enchanter's spells,
And I am free.

Now in the haven of untroubled rest
I land at last,
The hunger, and the thirst, and weary quest
For ever past.
There, Lord, to lose, in bliss of Thine embrace
The recreant will;
There, in the radiance of Thy blessed Face,
Be hushed and still;
There, speechless at Thy pierced Feet
See none and nought beside,
And know but this—that Thou art sweet,
That I am satisfied.

—GERHARD TERSTEEGEN, 1697-1769
Tr. Unknown

DELIGHTING IN GOD'S PRESENCE

GOD IS PRESENT EVERYWHERE

They who seek the throne of grace
Find that throne in every place;
If we live a life of prayer,
God is present everywhere.

In our sickness and our health,
In our want, or in our wealth,
If we look to God in prayer,
God is present everywhere.

When our earthly comforts fail,
When the woes of life prevail,
'Tis the time for earnest prayer;
God is present everywhere.

Then, my soul, in every strait,
To thy Father come, and wait;
He will answer every prayer:
God is present everywhere.

—OLIVER HOLDEN, 1765-1844

THE ROYAL PRIESTHOOD

The race of God's anointed priests
Shall never pass away;
Before His glorious face they stand,
And serve Him night and day.
Though reason raves, and unbelief
Flows on, a mighty flood,
There are, and shall be till the end,
The hidden priests of God.

His chosen souls, their earthly dross
Consumed in sacred fire,
To God's own heart their hearts ascend
In flame of deep desire;
The incense of their worship fills
His Temple's holiest place;
Their song with wonder fills the Heavens,
The glad new song of grace.

—*GERHARD TERSTEEGEN, 1697-1769*
Tr. Unknown

GOD REVEALS HIS PRESENCE

God reveals His presence:
Let us now adore Him,
And with awe appear before Him.
God is in His temple:
All within keep silence,
Prostrate lie with deepest reverence.
Him alone
God we own,
Him our God and Saviour:
Praise His Name for ever!

God reveals His presence:
Hear the harps resounding;
See the crowds the throne surrounding;
"Holy, holy, holy!"

Hear the hymn ascending,
Angels, saints, their voices blending.
Bow Thine ear
To us here;
Hearken, O Lord Jesus,
To our meaner praises.

O Thou Fount of blessing
Purify my spirit,
Trusting only in Thy merit:
Like the holy angels
Who behold Thy glory,
May I ceaselessly adore Thee.
Let Thy will
Ever still
Rule Thy Church terrestrial,
As the hosts celestial.

—GERHARD TERSTEEGEN, 1697-1769
Composite translation

WITHIN THE HOLY PLACE

His priest am I, before Him day and night,
Within His Holy Place;
And death, and life, and all things dark and bright,
I spread before His Face.
Rejoicing with His joy, yet ever still,
For silence is my song;
My work to bend beneath His blessed will,
All day, and all night long—
For ever holding with Him converse sweet,
Yet speechless, for my gladness is complete.

—GERHARD TERSTEEGEN, 1697-1769
Tr. Unknown

LO, GOD IS HERE!

Lo, God is here! let us adore,
And own how dreadful is this place;
Let all within us feel His power,
And silent bow before His face;
Who know His power, His grace who prove,
Serve Him with awe, with reverence love.

Lo, God is here! Him day and night
United choirs of angels sing;
To Him, enthroned above all height,
Heaven's host their noblest praises bring;
Disdain not, Lord, our meaner song,
Who praise Thee with a stammering tongue.

Being of beings, may our praise
Thy courts with grateful fragrance fill;
Still may we stand before Thy face,
Still hear and do Thy sovereign will;
To Thee may all our thoughts arise,
Ceaseless, accepted sacrifice.

—GERHARD TERSTEEGEN, 1697-1769
Tr. JOHN WESLEY, 1703-1791

ALLURED INTO THE DESERT

Allured into the desert,
With God alone, apart,
There spirit meeteth spirit,
There speaketh heart to heart.
Far, far on that untrodden shore,
God's secret place I find;
Alone I pass the golden door,
The dearest left behind.

There God and I—none other;
Oh far from men to be!
Nay, midst the crowd and tumult,

Still, Lord, alone with Thee.
Still folded close upon Thy breast,
In field, and mart, and street,
Untroubled in that perfect rest,
That isolation sweet.

O God, Thou art far other
Than men have dreamed and taught,
Unspoken in all language,
Unpictured in all thought.
Thou God art God—he only learns
What that great Name must be,
Whose raptured heart within him burns,
Because he walks with Thee.

Stilled by that wondrous Presence,
That tenderest embrace,
The years of longing over,
Do we behold Thy Face;
We seek no more than Thou hast given,
We ask no vision fair,
Thy precious Blood has opened Heaven,
And we have found Thee there.

O weary souls, draw near Him;
To you I can but bring
One drop of that great ocean,
One blossom of that spring;
Sealed with His kiss, my lips are dumb,
My soul with awe is still;
Let him that is athirst but come,
And freely drink his fill.

—GERHARD TERSTEEGEN, 1697-1769
Tr. Unknown

THE RAPTURES OF DIVINE LOVE

O LOVE DIVINE!

O Love Divine! that stoop'st to share
Our sharpest pang, our bitterest tear,
On Thee we cast each earth-born care,
We smile at pain while Thou art near.

Though long the weary way we tread,
And sorrow crown each lingering year,
No path we shun, no darkness dread,
Our hearts still whispering, "Thou art near."

When drooping pleasure turns to grief,
And trembling faith is changed to fear,
The murmuring wind, the quivering leaf,
Shall softly tell us Thou art near.

On Thee we cast our burdening woe,
O Love Divine, for ever dear;
Content to suffer while we know,
Living or dying, Thou art near!

—*OLIVER WENDELL HOLMES, 1809-1894*

I LOVE MY GOD

I love my God, but with no love of mine,
For I have none to give;
I love thee, Lord; but all the love is Thine,
For by Thy life I live.
I am as nothing, and rejoice to be
Emptied, and lost, and swallowed up in Thee.

Thou, Lord, alone, art all Thy children need,
And there is none beside;
From Thee the streams of blessedness proceed
In Thee the blest abide, —
Fountain of life, and all-abounding grace,
Our source, our center, and our dwelling-place.

—*JEANNE MARIE DE LA MOTTE-GUYON, 1648-1717*
Tr. Unknown

THE ACQUIESCENCE OF PURE LOVE

Love! if thy destined sacrifice am I,
Come, slay thy victim, and prepare Thy fires;
Plunged in Thy depths of mercy, let me die
The death which every soul that lives desires.

I watch my hours, and see them fleet away;
The time is long that I have languished here;
Yet all my thoughts Thy purposes obey,
With no reluctance, cheerful and sincere.

To me 'tis equal, whether Love ordain
My life or death, appoint me pain or ease;
My soul perceives no real ill in pain;
In ease or health no real good she sees.

One good she covets, and that good alone,
To choose Thy will, from selfish bias free;
And to prefer a cottage to a throne,
And grief to comfort, if it pleases Thee.

That we should bear the cross is Thy command,
Die to the world, and live to self no more;
Suffer, unmoved, beneath the rudest hand;
When shipwrecked pleased as when upon the shore.

—*JEANNE MARIE DE LA MOTTE-GUYON, 1648-1717*
Tr. Unknown

JESUS, THY BOUNDLESS LOVE TO ME

Jesus, Thy boundless love to me
No thought can reach, no tongue declare;
O knit my thankful heart to Thee,
And reign without a rival there:
Thine wholly, Thine alone I am:
Be Thou alone my constant flame.

O grant that nothing in my soul
May dwell, but Thy pure love alone;
O may Thy love possess me whole,
My joy, my treasure, and my crown:
Strange fires far from my soul remove;
May every act, word, thought, be love.

O Love, how cheering is Thy ray;
All pain before Thy presence flies;
Care, anguish, sorrow, melt away,
Where'er Thy healing beams arise;
O Jesus, nothing may I see,
Nothing desire, or seek, but Thee.

In suffering, be Thy love my peace;
In weakness, be Thy love my power;
And, when the storms of life shall cease,
Jesus, in that important hour,
In death, as life, be Thou my guide,
And save me, who for me hast died.

—*PAUL GERHARDT, 1607-1676*
Tr. John Wesley, 1703-1791

O LOVE DIVINE!

O Love divine, how sweet Thou art!
When shall I find my willing heart
All taken up by Thee?
I thirst, I faint, I die to prove
The greatness of redeeming love,—
The love of Christ to me.

Stronger His love than death or hell;
Its riches are unsearchable;
The first-born sons of light
Desire in vain its depths to see;
They cannot reach the mystery,
The length, the breadth, the height.

God only knows the love of God;
O that it now were shed abroad
In this poor stony heart:
For love I sigh, for love I pine;
This only portion, Lord, be mine;
Be mine this better part.

O that I could forever sit
With Mary at the Master's feet!
Be this my happy choice;
My only care, delight, and bliss,
My joy, my heaven on earth, be this,
To hear the Bridegroom's voice.

O that I could, with favor'd John,
Recline my weary head upon
The dear Redeemer's breast:
From care, and sin, and sorrow free,
Give me, O Lord, to find in Thee
My everlasting rest.

—CHARLES WESLEY, 1707-1788

THE HIDDEN LOVE OF GOD

Thou hidden Love of God, whose height,
Whose depth unfathomed, no man knows,
I see from far Thy beauteous light,
Inly I sigh for Thy repose;
My heart is pained, nor can it be
At rest till it finds rest in Thee.

Thy secret voice invites me still
The sweetness of Thy yoke to prove;
And fain I would; but, though my will
Seem fixed, yet wide my passions rove.
Yet hindrances strew all the way;
I aim at Thee, yet from Thee stray.

'Tis mercy all, that Thou hast brought
My mind to seek her peace in Thee;
Yet, while I seek but find Thee not,
No peace my wandering soul shall see.
O when shall all my wanderings end,
And all my steps to Thee-ward tend?

Is there a thing beneath the sun
That strives with Thee my heart to share?
Ah! tear it thence, and reign alone,
The Lord of every motion there;
Then shall my heart from earth be free,
When it hath found repose in Thee.

—*GERHARD TERSTEEGEN, 1697-1769*
Tr. John Wesley, 1703-1791

LOVE'S IMMENSITY

O past and gone!
How great is God! how small am I!
A mote in the illimitable sky,
Amidst the glory deep, and wide, and high
Of Heaven's unclouded sun.
There to forget myself for evermore;
Lost, swallowed up in Love's immensity,
The sea that knows no sounding and no shore,
God only there, not I.

More near than I unto myself can be,
Art Thou to me;
So have I lost myself in finding Thee,
Have lost myself for ever, O my Sun!
The boundless Heaven of Thine eternal love
Around me, and beneath me, and above;
In glory of that golden day
The former things are passed away—
I, past and gone.

—*GERHARD TERSTEEGEN, 1697-1769*

The Rest of Faith

ALL MUST BE WELL

Through the love of God our Saviour,
All will be well;
Free and changeless is His favor,
All, all is well;
Precious is the blood that heard us,
Perfect is the grace that seed us,
Strong the hand stretch'd out to shield us,
All must be well.

Though we pass through tribulation,
All will be well;
Ours is such a full salvation,
All, all is well;
Happy, still in God confiding,
Fruitful, if in Christ abiding
Holy, through the Spirit's guiding,
All must be well.

We expect a bright tomorrow,
All will be well;
Faith can sing, through days of sorrow,
All, all is well;
On our Father's love relying,
Jesus ev'ry need supplying,
Or in living or in dying,
All must be well.

—*MARY BOWLEY PETERS, 1813-1856*

CONFIDENCE

If thou but suffer God to guide thee,
And hope in Him through all thy ways,
He'll give thee strength, whate'er betide thee,
And bear thee through the evil days;
Who trusts in God's unchanging love
Builds on the rock that nought can move.

What can these anxious cares avail thee,
These never-ceasing moans and sighs?
What can it help if thou bewail thee
O'er each dark moment as it flies?
Our cross and trials do but press
The heavier for our bitterness.

Only be still, and wait His leisure
In cheerful hope, with heart content
To take whate'er thy Father's pleasure
And all-discerning love hath sent;
Nor doubt our inmost wants are known
To Him who chose us for His own.

Sing, pray, and keep His ways unswerving;
So do thine own part faithfully,
And trust His word,—though undeserving,
Thou yet shalt find it true for thee;
God never yet forsook at need
The soul that trusted Him indeed.

—*GEORGE C. NEUMARK, 1621-1681*
Tr. Catherine Winkworth, 1829-1878

SOMETIMES A LIGHT SURPRISES

Sometimes a light surprises
The Christian while he sings;
It is the Lord, who rises
With healing in His wings:
When comforts are declining,
He grants the soul again
A season of clear shining,
To cheer it after rain.

In holy contemplation,
We sweetly then pursue
The theme of God's salvation,
And find it ever new:
Set free from present sorrow,
We cheerfully can say,
"E'en let the unknown morrow
Bring with it what it may."

It can bring with it nothing,
But He will bear us through;
Who gives the lilies clothing,
Will clothe His people too:
Beneath the spreading heavens,
No creature but is fed;
And He who feeds the ravens
Will give His children bread.

—WILLIAM COWPER, 1731-1800

THE BLESSED JOURNEY

Let Him lead thee blindfold onwards,
Love needs not to know;
Children whom the Father leadeth
Ask not where they go.
Though the path be all unknown,
Over moors and mountains lone.

Give no ear to reason's questions;
Let the blind man hold
That the sun is but a fable
Men believed of old.
At the breast the babe will grow;
Whence the milk he need not know.

—GERHARD TERSTEEGEN, 1697-1769
Tr. Unknown

JESUS, I AM RESTING, RESTING

Jesus, I am resting, resting
In the joy of what Thou art,
I am finding out the greatness
Of Thy loving heart.
Here I gaze and gaze upon Thee,
As Thy beauty fills my soul,
For by Thy transforming power,
Thou hast made me whole.

O how great Thy loving-kindness,
Vaster, broader than the sea;
O how marvellous Thy goodness
Lavished all on me—
Yes, I rest in Thee, Beloved,
Know what wealth of grace is Thine,
Know Thy certainty of promise
And have made it mine.

Simply trusting Thee, Lord Jesus,
I behold Thee as Thou art,
And Thy love, so pure, so changeless,
Satisfies my heart,
Satisfies its deepest longing,
Meets, supplies my every need,
Compasseth me round with blessings:
Thine is love indeed.

Ever lift Thy face upon me
As I work and wait for Thee;
Resting 'neath Thy smile, Lord Jesus,
Earth's dark shadows flee.
Brightness of my Father's glory,
Sunshine of my Father's face,
Let Thy glory e'er shine on me,
Fill me with Thy grace.

—JEAN SOPHIA PIGOTT, 19th Century

RESIGNATION

A little bird I am,
Shut from the fields of air;
And in my cage I sit and sing
To Him who placed me there;
Well pleased a prisoner to be,
Because, my God, it pleases Thee.

Naught have I else to do;
I sing the whole day long;
And He whom most I love to please
Doth listen to my song;
He caught and bound my wandering wing,
But still He bends to hear me sing.

Thou hast an ear to hear,
A heart to love and bless;
And though my notes were e'er so rude,
Thou wouldst not hear the less;
Because Thou knowest, as they fall,
That love, sweet love, inspires them all.

My cage confines me round;
Abroad I cannot fly;
But though my wing is closely bound,
My heart's at liberty.
My prison walls cannot control
The flight, the freedom, of the soul.

O, it is good to soar
These bolts and bars above,
To Him whose purpose I adore,
Whose providence I love;
And in Thy mighty will to find
The joy, the freedom, of the mind.

—JEANNE MARIE DE LA MOTTE-GUYON, 1648-1717
Tr. Unknown

IN HEAVENLY LOVE ABIDING

In heavenly love abiding,
No change my heart shall fear;
And safe is such confiding,
For nothing changes here:
The storm may roar without me,
My heart may low be laid;
But God is round about me,
And can I be dismayed?

Wherever He may guide me,
No want shall turn me back;
My Shepherd is beside me,
And nothing can I lack.
His wisdom ever waketh,
His sight is never dim:
He knows the way He taketh,
And I will walk with Him.

Green pastures are before me,
Which yet I have not seen;
Bright skies will soon be o'er me,
Where the dark clouds have been.
My hope I cannot measure:
My path to life is free:
My Saviour has my treasure,
And He will walk with me.

—ANNA LAETITIA WARING, 1820-1910

THE REMEMBRANCE OF MERCY

Why art thou sorrowful, servant of God?
And what is this dullness that hangs o'er thee now?
Sing the praises of Jesus, and sing them aloud,
And the song shall dispel the dark cloud from thy brow.

For is there a thought in the wide world so sweet,
As that God has so cared for us, bad as we are,
That He thinks of us, plans for us, stoops to entreat,
And follows us, wander we ever so far?

Then how can the heart e'er be drooping or sad,
Which God hath once touched with the light of His grace?
Can the child have a doubt who but lately hath laid
Himself to repose in his father's embrace?

And is it not wonderful, servant of God!
That He should have honoured us so with His love,
That the sorrows of life should but shorten the road
Which leads to Himself and the mansion above?

Oh then when the spirit of darkness comes down
With clouds and uncertainties into thy heart,
One look to thy Saviour, one thought of thy crown,
And the tempest is over, the shadows depart.

That God hath once whispered a word in thine ear,
Or sent thee from heaven one sorrow for sin,
Is enough for a life both to banish all fear,
And to turn into peace all the troubles within.

The schoolmen can teach thee far less about heaven,
Of the height of God's power, or the depth of His love,
Than the fire in thy heart when thy sin was forgiven,
Or the light that one mercy brings down from above.

Then why dost thou weep so? For see how time flies,
The time that for loving and praising was given!
Away with thee, child, then, and hide thy red eyes

In the lap, the kind lap, of thy Father in heaven.

—FREDERICK WILLIAM FABER, 1814-1863

The Spiritual Warfare

DISTRACTIONS IN PRAYER

Ah dearest Lord! I cannot pray,
My fancy is not free;
Unmannerly distractions come,
And force my thoughts from Thee.

The world that looks so dull all day
Glows bright on me at prayer,
And plans that ask no thought but then
Wake up and meet me there.

All nature one full fountain seems
Of dreamy sight and sound,
Which, when I kneel, breaks up its deeps,
And makes a deluge round.

Old voices murmur in my ear,
New hopes start to life,
And past and future gaily blend
In one bewitching strife.

My very flesh has restless fits;
My changeful limbs conspire
With all these phantoms of the mind
My inner self to tire.

I cannot pray; yet, Lord! Thou knowst
The pain it is to me
To have my vainly struggling thoughts
Thus torn away from Thee.

Sweet Jesus! teach me how to prize
These tedious hours when I,
Foolish and mute before Thy Face,
In helpless worship lie.

Prayer was not meant for luxury,
Or selfish pastime sweet;
It is the prostrate creature's place
At his Creator's Feet.

Had I, dear Lord! no pleasure found
But in the thought of Thee,
Prayer would have come unsought, and been
A truer liberty.

Yet Thou art oft most present, Lord!
In weak distracted prayer:
A sinner out of heart with self
Most often finds Thee there.

For prayer that humbles sets the soul
From all illusions free,
And teaches it how utterly,
Dear Lord! it hangs on Thee.

The heart, that on self-sacrifice
Is covetously bent,
Will bless Thy chastening hand that makes
Its prayer its punishment.

My Saviour! why should I complain
And why fear aught but sin?
Distractions are but outward things;
Thy peace dwells far within.

These surface-troubles come and go,
Like rufflings of the sea;
The deeper depth is out of reach
To all, my God, but Thee.

—FREDERIC WILLIAM FABER, 1814-1863

THE BENEFITS OF SUFFERING

By sufferings only can we know
The nature of the life we live;
The temper of our souls they show,
How true, how pure, the love we give.
To leave my love in doubt would be
No less disgrace than misery!

I welcome, then, with heart sincere,
The cross my Saviour bids me take;
No load, no trial, is severe,
That's borne or suffered for His sake:
And thus my sorrow shall proclaim
A love that's worthy of the name.

—JEANNE MARIE DE LA MOTTE-GUYON, 1648-1717
Tr. Unknown

SORROW AND LOVE

Self-love no grace in sorrow sees,
Consults her own peculiar ease,
'Tis all the bliss she knows;
But nobler aims true Love employ,
In self-denial is her joy,
In suffering her repose.

Sorrow and Love go side by side;
Nor height nor depth can e'er divide
Their heaven-appointed bands;
Those dear associates still are one,
Nor, till the race of life is run,
Disjoin their wedded hands.

Thy choice and mine shall be the same,
Inspirer of that holy flame,
Which must forever blaze!
To take the cross and follow Thee,
Where love and duty lead, shall be
My portion and my praise.

—*JEANNE MARIE DE LA MOTTE-GUYON, 1648-1717*
Tr. Unknown

Victory Through Praise

COME, O MY SOUL

Come, O my soul, in sacred lays,
Attempt thy great Creator's praise:
But, oh, what tongue can speak His fame!
What mortal verse can reach the theme!

Enthroned amid the radiant spheres,
He glory like a garment wears;
To form a robe of light divine,
Ten thousand suns around Him shine.

In all our Maker's grand designs,
Omnipotence, with wisdom, shines;
His works, through all this wondrous frame,
Declare the glory of His Name.

Raised on devotion's lofty wing,
Do thou, my soul, His glories sing;
And let His praise employ thy tongue,
Till listening worlds shall join the song!

—*THOMAS BLACKLOCK, 18th Century*

BLESS, O MY SOUL, THE LIVING GOD

Bless, O my soul, the living God,
Call home thy thoughts that rove abroad;
Let all the pow'rs within me join
In work and worship so divine.

Bless, O my soul, the God of grace;
His favors claim thy highest praise;
Why should the wonders He hath wrought
Be lost in silence, and forgot?

'Tis He, my soul, that sent His Son
To die for crimes which thou hast done;
He owns the ransom, and forgives
The hourly follies of our lives.

Let the whole earth His power confess,
Let the whole earth adore His grace;
The Gentile with the Jew shall join
In work and worship so divine.

—ISAAC WATTS, 1674-1748
After Psalm 103

I'LL PRAISE MY MAKER

I'll praise my Maker while I've breath,
And when my voice is lost in death,
Praise shall employ my nobler powers;
My days of praise shall ne'er be past,
While life, and thought, and being last,
Or immortality endures.

Happy the man whose hopes rely
On Israel's God; He made the sky,
And earth, and seas, with all their train;
His truth for ever stands secure,
He saves the opprest, He feeds the poor,
And none shall find His promise vain.

The Lord pours eyesight on the blind;
The Lord supports the fainting mind;
He sends the labouring conscience peace;
He helps the stranger in distress,
The widow and the fatherless,
And grants the prisoner sweet release.

I'll praise Him while He lends me breath,
And when my voice is lost in death,
Praise shall employ my nobler powers;
My days of praise shall ne'er be past,
While life, and thought, and being last,
Or immortality endures.

—ISSAC WATTS, 1674-1748
Al. John Wesley, 1703-1791

I SING TH' ALMIGHTY POWER OF GOD

I sing th' almighty power of God,
That made the mountains rise,
That spread the flowing seas abroad,
And built the lofty skies.

I sing the wisdom that ordained
The sun to rule the day;
The moon shines full at His command,
And all the stars obey.

I sing the goodness of the Lord,
That filled the earth with food;
He formed the creatures with His word,
And then pronounced them good.

Lord! how Thy wonders are displayed
Where'er I turn mine eye!
If I survey the ground I tread,
Or gaze upon the sky!

There's not a plant or flower below
But makes Thy glories known;
And clouds arise, and tempests blow,
By order from Thy throne.

Creatures that borrow life from Thee
Are subject to Thy care;
There's not a place where we can flee
But God is present there.

—ISAAC WATTS, 1674-1748

NOW THANK WE ALL OUR GOD

Now thank we all our God,
With heart, and hands, and voices,
Who wondrous things hath done,
In whom His world rejoices;
Who from our mother's arms
Hath blessed us on our way
With countless gifts of love,
And still is ours today.

O may this bounteous God
Through all our life be near us,
With ever joyful hearts
And blessed peace to cheer us;
And keep us in His grace,
And guide us when perplexed,
And free us from all ills
In this world and the next.

All praise and thanks to God
The Father now be given,
The Son, and Him who reigns
With them in highest heaven,
The one eternal God,
Whom earth and heaven adore;
For thus it was, is now,
And shall be evermore.

—MARTIN RINCKART, 1586-1649
Tr. Catharine Winkworth, 1829-1878

TE DEUM LAUDAMUS

We praise Thee, O God,
we acknowledge Thee to be the Lord.
All the earth doth worship Thee, the Father everlasting.
To Thee all angels cry aloud, the heavens and all the powers therein;
To Thee Cherubim and Seraphim continually do cry,
Holy, holy, holy, Lord God of Sabaoth:
Heaven and earth are full of the majesty of Thy glory.
The glorious company of the Apostles praise Thee.
The goodly fellowship of the Prophets praise Thee.
The noble army of Martyrs praise Thee.
The holy Church throughout all the world doth acknowledge Thee,
The Father of an infinite Majesty;
Thine adorable, true and only Son;
Also the Holy Ghost, the Comforter.

Thou art the King of Glory, O Christ;
Thou art the everlasting Son of the Father.
When Thou tookest upon Thee to deliver man
Thou didst humble Thyself to be born of a virgin.
When Thou hadst overcome the sharpness of death
Thou didst open the kingdom of heaven to all believers.
Thou sittest at the right hand of God in the glory of the Father.
We believe that Thou shalt come to be our Judge.
We therefore pray Thee help Thy servants whom
Thou hast redeemed with Thy precious blood.
Make them to be numbered with Thy saints in glory everlasting.

O Lord, save Thy people, and bless Thine heritage.
Govern them, and lift them up forever.
Day by day we magnify Thee,
And we worship Thy Name forever, world without end.
Vouchsafe, O Lord, to keep us this day without sin.
O Lord, have mercy upon us, have mercy upon us.
O Lord, let Thy mercy be upon us, as our trust is in Thee.
O Lord, in Thee have I trusted, let me never be confounded.

THE PRAYER OF QUIET

THE SPIRIT OF PRAYER

The prayers I make will then be sweet indeed
If Thou the Spirit give by which I pray:
My unassisted heart is barren clay,
That of its native self can nothing feed:
Of good and pious works Thou art the seed,
That quickens only where Thou say'st it may:
Unless Thou show to us Thine own true way
No man can find it: Father! Thou must lead.
Do Thou, then, breathe those thoughts into my mind
By which such virtue may in me be bred
That in Thy holy footsteps I may tread;
The fetters of my tongue do Thou unbind,
That I may have the power to sing of Thee,
And sound Thy praises everlastingly.

—FROM THE ITALIAN OF MICHAEL ANGELO, 1475-1564
Tr. William Wordsworth, 1770-1850

MY GOD! SILENT TO THEE!

As, down in the sunless retreats of the ocean,
Sweet flowers are springing no mortal can see,
So, deep in my heart, the still prayer of devotion,
Unheard by the world, rises, silent, to Thee,
My God! silent, to Thee,—

Pure, warm, silent, to Thee.
As still to the star of its worship, though clouded,
The needle points faithfully o'er the dim sea,
So, dark as I roam, thro' this wintry world shrouded,
The hope of my spirit turns, trembling, to Thee,
My God! trembling, to Thee,—
True, fond, trembling, to Thee.

—THOMAS MOORE, 1719-1852

GOD'S ETERNAL NOW

Stillness midst the ever-changing,
Lord, my rest art Thou;
So for me has dawned the morning,
God's eternal NOW.
Now for me the day unsetting,
Now the song begun;
Now, the deep surpassing glory,
Brighter than the sun.

Hail! all hail! thou peaceful country
Of eternal calm;
Summer land of milk and honey,
Where the streams are balm.
There the Lord my Shepherd leads me,
Wheresoe'er He will;
In the fresh green pastures feeds me,
By the waters still.

Well I know them, those still waters!
Peace and rest at last;
In their depths the quiet heavens
Tell the storms are past,
Nought to mar the picture fair,
Of the glory resting there.

—GERHARD TERSTEEGEN, 1697-1769
Tr. Unknown

MY HEART IS RESTING, O MY GOD

My heart is resting, O my God,
I will give thanks and sing;
My heart is at the secret source
Of every precious thing.
Now the frail vessel Thou hast made
No hand but Thine shall fill;
For the waters of the earth have failed,
And I am thirsty still.

I thirst for springs of heavenly life,
And here all day they rise;
I seek the treasure of Thy love,
And close at hand it lies.
And a new song is in my mouth
To long-loved music set:
"Glory to Thee for all the grace
I have not tasted yet;

"Glory to Thee for strength withheld,
For want and weakness known;
And the fear that sends me to Thy breast
For what is most my own."
I have a heritage of joy
That yet I must not see;
But the hand that bled to make it mine
Is keeping it for me.

My heart is resting, O my God,
My heart is in Thy care;
I hear the voice of joy and health
Resounding everywhere.
"Thou art my portion," saith my soul,
Ten thousand voices say,
And the music of their glad Amen
Will never die away.

—*ANNA LAETITIA WARING, 1820-1910*

HIDDEN IN GOD'S HEART

How good it is, when weaned from all beside,
With God alone the soul is satisfied,
Deep hidden in His heart!
How good it is, redeemed, and washed, and shriven,
To dwell, a cloistered soul, with Christ in heaven,
Joined, never more to part!

How good the heart's still chamber thus to close
On all but God alone—
There in the sweetness of His love repose,
His love unknown!
All else for ever lost—forgotten all
That else can be;
In rapture undisturbed, O Lord, to fall
And worship Thee.

No place, no time, 'neath those eternal skies—
How still, how sweet, and how surpassing fair
That solitude in glades of Paradise,
And, as in olden days, God walking there.
I hear His voice amidst the stillness blest,
And care and fear are past—
I lay me down within His arms to rest
From all my works at last.

How good it is when from the distant land,
From lonely wanderings, and from weary ways,
The soul hath reached at last the golden strand,
The Gates of Praise!
There, where the tide of endless love flows free,
There, in the sweet and glad eternity,
The still, unfading Now.
Ere yet the days and nights of earth are o'er,
Begun the day that is for evermore—
Such rest art Thou!

—*GERHARD TERSTEEGEN, 1697-1769*
Tr. Unknown

THE BLISS OF COMMUNION

THE DISCIPLE TO HIS LORD

Teach me to do the thing that pleaseth Thee;
Thou art my God, in Thee I live and move;
Oh, let Thy loving Spirit lead me forth
Into the land of righteousness and love.

Thy love the law and impulse of my soul,
Thy righteousness its fitness and its plea,
Thy loving Spirit mercy's sweet control
To make me liker, draw me nearer Thee.

My highest hope to be where, Lord, Thou art,
To lose myself in Thee my richest gain,
To do Thy will the habit of my heart,
To grieve the Spirit my severest pain.

Thy smile my sunshine, all my peace from thence,
From self alone what could that peace destroy?
Thy joy my sorrow at the least offence,
My sorrow that I am not more Thy joy.

—*JOHN S. B. MONSELL, 1811-1875*

JOY IN THE PRESENCE OF JESUS

How tedious and tasteless the hours
When Jesus no longer I see!
Sweet prospects, sweet birds, and sweet flowers,
Have all lost their sweetness to me;-

The midsummer sun shines but dim,
The fields strive in vain to look gay;
But when I am happy in Him,
December's as pleasant as May.

His Name yields the richest perfume,
And sweeter than music His voice;
His presence disperses my gloom,
And makes all within me rejoice;

I should, were He always thus nigh,
Have nothing to wish or to fear;
No mortal so happy as I,
My summer would last all the year.

Content with beholding His face,
My all to His pleasure resign'd,
No changes of season or place
Would make any change in my mind:

While blest with a sense of His love,
A palace a toy would appear;
And prisons would palaces prove,
If Jesus would dwell with me there.

My Lord, if indeed I am Thine,
If Thou art my sun and my song,
Say, why do I languish and pine?
And why are my winters so long?

O drive these dark clouds from my sky;
Thy soul-cheering presence restore;
Or take me to Thee up on high,
Where winter and clouds are no more.

—JOHN NEWTON, 1725-1807

O JESUS, KING MOST WONDERFUL

O Jesus, King most wonderful,
Thou Conqueror renowned,
Thou Sweetness most ineffable,
In whom all joys are found!

When once Thou visitest the heart,
Then truth begins to shine,
Then earthly vanities depart,
Then kindles love divine.

O Jesus, Light of all below!
Thou Fount of life and fire!
Surpassing all the joys we know,
And all we can desire,—

May every heart confess Thy Name,
And ever Thee adore,
And, seeking Thee, itself inflame
To seek Thee more and more.

Thee may our tongues for ever bless,
Thee may we love alone,
And ever in our lives express
The image of Thine own.

—*BERNARD OF CLAIRVAUX, 1091-1153*
Tr. Edward Caswall, 1814-1878

CHRIST OUR LIGHT

O Christ our Light, Whom even in darkness we
(So we look up) discern and gaze upon,
O Christ, Thou loveliest Light that ever shone,
Thou Light of Light, Fount of all lights that be,
Grant us clear vision of Thy Light to see,
Tho' other lights elude us, or begone
Into the secret of oblivion,
Or gleam in places higher than man's degree.

Who looks on Thee looks full on his desire
Who looks on Thee looks full on Very Love:
Looking, he answers well, "What lack I yet?"
His heat and cold wait not on earthly fire,
His wealth is not of earth to lose or get;
Earth reels, but he has stored his store above.

—CHRISTINA ROSSETTI, 1830-1894

AS OINTMENT POURED FORTH

Is this that Name as ointment poured forth
For which the virgins love Thee; King of kings
And Lord of lords? All seraphs clad in wings;
All Cherubs and all Wheels which south and north,
Which east and west turn not in going forth;
All many-semblanced ordered spirits, as rings
Of rainbow in unwonted fashionings,
Might answer, Yes. But we from south and north,
From east and west, a feeble folk who came
By desert ways in quest of land unseen,
A promised land of pasture ever green
And ever springing ever singing wave,
Know best Thy Name of Jesus: Blessed Name,
Man's life and resurrection from the grave.

—CHRISTINA ROSSETTI, 1830-1894

O! TELL ME, THOU LIFE AND DELIGHT OF MY SOUL!

O! tell me, Thou life and delight of my soul,
Where the flock of Thy pastures are feeding;
I seek Thy protection, I need Thy control,
I would go where my Shepherd is leading.

O! tell me the place where Thy flocks are at rest,
Where the noontide will find them reposing?
The tempest now rages, my soul is distress'd,
And the pathway of peace I am losing.

O! why should I stray with the flocks of Thy foes,
'Mid the desert where now they are roving,
Where hunger and thirst, where affliction and woes,
And temptations their ruin are proving!

O! when shall my foes and my wandering cease?
And the follies that fill me with weeping!
Thou Shepherd of Israel, restore me that peace
Thou dost give to the flock Thou art keeping.

A voice from the Shepherd now bids thee return
By the way where the footprints are lying:
No longer to wander, no longer to mourn;
O fair one, now homeward be flying!

—THOMAS HASTINGS, 1784-1872

THE FACE OF CHRIST

A rose, a lily, and the Face of Christ
Have all our hearts sufficed:
For He is Rose of Sharon nobly born,
Our Rose without a thorn;
And He is Lily of the Valley, He
Most sweet in purity.
But when we come to name Him as He is,
Godhead, Perfection, Bliss,
All tongues fall silent, while pure hearts alone
Complete their orison.

—CHRISTINA ROSSETTI, 1830-1894

CHRIST, WHOSE GLORY FILLS THE SKIES

Christ, whose glory fills the skies,
Christ, the true, the only light,
Sun of Righteousness, arise!
Triumph o'er the shades of night;
Day-spring from on high, be near!
Day-star, in my heart appear!

Dark and cheerless is the morn,
If Thy life is hid from me;
Joyless is the day's return,
Till Thy mercy's beams I see;
Till they inward light impart,
Warmth and gladness to my heart.

Visit, then, this soul of mine;
Pierce the gloom of sin and grief;
Fill me, radiant Sun divine;
Scatter all my unbelief;
More and more Thyself display,
Shining to the perfect day.

—CHARLES WESLEY, 1707-1788

JESU, HIGHEST HEAVEN'S COMPLETENESS

Jesu, highest heaven's completeness,
Name of music to the ear,
To the lips surpassing sweetness,
Wine the fainting heart to cheer.

Eating Thee, the soul may hunger,
Drinking, still athirst may be;
But for earthly food no longer,
Nor for any stream but Thee.

Jesu, all delight exceeding,
Only hope of heart distrest;
Weeping eyes and spirit mourning
Find in Thee a place of rest.

Stay, O Beauty uncreated,
Ever ancient, ever new;
Banish deeds of darkness hated,
With Thy sweetness all bedew.

Jesu, fairest blossom springing
From a maiden ever pure,
May our lips Thy praise be singing
While eternal years endure.

—*BERNARD OF CLAIRVAUX, 1091-1153*
Tr. Robert Campbell, 1814-1888

SHOW ME THY FACE

Show me Thy face—one transient gleam
Of loveliness divine,
And I shall never think or dream
Of other love save Thine:
All lesser light will darken quite,
All lower glories wane,
The beautiful of earth will scarce
Seem beautiful again.

Show me Thy face—my faith and love
Shall henceforth fixed be,
And nothing here have power to move
My soul's serenity.
My life shall seem a trance, a dream,
And all I feel and see,
Illusive, visionary—Thou
The one reality!

Show me Thy face—I shall forget
The weary days of yore,
The fretting ghosts of vain regret
Shall haunt my soul no more.
All doubts and fears for future years
In quiet trust subside,
And naught but blest content and calm
Within my breast abide.

Show me Thy face—the heaviest cross
Will then seem light to bear;
There will be gain in every loss,
And peace with every care.
With such light feet the years will fleet,
Life seem as brief as blest,
Till I have laid my burden down,
And entered into rest.

—AUTHOR UNKNOWN

NONE OTHER LAMB, NONE OTHER NAME

None other Lamb, none other Name,
None other Hope in heaven or earth or sea,
None other Hiding-place from guilt and shame,
None beside Thee.

My faith burns low, my hope burns low;
Only my heart's desire cries out in me,
By the deep thunder of its want and woe,
Cries out to Thee.

Lord, Thou art Life, though I be dead;
Love's Fire Thou art, however cold I be:
Nor heaven have I, nor place to lay my head,
Nor home, but Thee.

—CHRLSTINA ROSSETTI, 1830-1894

ASPIRATIONS OF THE SOUL AFTER CHRIST

My Spouse! in whose presence I live,
Sole object of all my desires,
Who know'st what a flame I conceive,
And canst easily double its fires;
How pleasant is all that I meet!
From fear of adversity free,
I find even sorrow made sweet,
Because 'tis assign'd me by Thee.

Transported I see Thee display
Thy riches and glory divine;
I have only my life to repay,
Take what I would gladly resign.
Thy will is the treasure I seek,
For Thou art as faithful as strong;
There let me, obedient and meek,
Repose myself all the day long.

My spirit and faculties fail;
Oh finish what Love has begun!
Destroy what is sinful and frail,
And dwell in the soul Thou hast won!
Dear theme of my wonder and praise,
I cry, who is worthy as Thou!
I can only be silent and gaze;
'Tis all that is left to me now.

Oh glory, in which I am lost,
Too deep for the plummet of thought!
On an ocean of Deity toss'd,
I am swallow'd, I sink into nought.

Yet lost and absorb'd as I seem,
I chant to the praise of my King;
And though overwhelm'd by the theme,
Am happy whenever I sing.

—*JEANNE MARIE DE LA MOTTE-GUYON, 1648-1718*
Tr. Unknown

THE PAIN OF LOVE

Jesus! why dost Thou love me so?
What hast Thou seen in me
To make my happiness so great,
So dear a joy to Thee?

Wert Thou not God, I then might think
Thou hadst no eye to read
The badness of that selfish heart,
For which Thine own did bleed.

But Thou art God, and knowest all;
Dear Lord! Thou knowest me;
And yet Thy knowledge hinders not
Thy love's sweet liberty.

Ah, how Thy grace hath wooed my soul
With persevering wiles!
Now give me tears to weep; for tears
Are deeper joy than smiles.

Each proof renewed of Thy great love
Humbles me more and more,
And brings to light forgotten sins,
And lays them at my door.

The more I love Thee, Lord! the more
I hate my own cold heart;
The more Thou woundest me with love;
The more I feel the smart.

What shall I do, then, dearest Lord!
Say, shall I fly from Thee,
And hide my poor unloving self
Where Thou canst never see?

Or shall I pray that Thy dear love
To me might not be given?
Ah, no! love must be pain on earth,
If it be bliss in heaven.

—FREDERICK WILLIAM FABER, 1814-1863

THOU HIDDEN SOURCE OF CALM REPOSE

Thou hidden Source of calm repose,
Thou all-sufficient Love Divine,
My help and refuge from my foes,
Secure I am, if Thou art mine;
And lo! from sin, and grief, and shame,
I hide me, Jesus, in Thy Name.

Thy mighty Name salvation is,
And keeps my happy soul above;
Comfort it brings, and power, and peace,
And joy, and everlasting love;
To me, with Thy dear Name, are given
Pardon, and holiness, and heaven.

Jesus, my all in all Thou art;
My rest in toil, my ease in pain,
The medicine of my broken heart;
In war my peace, in loss my gain,
My smile beneath the tyrant's frown,
In shame my glory and my crown:

In want my plentiful supply,
In weakness my almighty power;
In bonds my perfect liberty,
My light in Satan's darkest hour;
My joy in grief, my shield in strife,
In death my everlasting life.

—CHARLES WESLEY, 1707-1788

THE MAN DIVINE

In the Paradise of glory
Is the Man Divine;
There my heart, O God, is tasting
Fellowship with Thine.

Called to share Thy joy unmeasured,
Now is heaven begun;
I rejoice with Thee, O Father,
In Thy glorious Son.

Where the heart of God is resting,
I have found my rest;
Christ who found me in the desert,
Laid me on His breast.

There in deep unhindered fulness
Doth my joy flow free—
On through everlasting ages,
Lord, beholding Thee.

Round me is creation groaning,
Death, and sin, and care;
But there is a rest remaining,
And my Lord is there.

There I find a blessed stillness
In His courts of love;
All below but strife and darkness,
Cloudless peace above.

'Tis a solitary pathway
To that fair retreat—
Where in deep and sweet communion
Sit I at His feet.

In that glorious isolation,
Loneliness how blest,
From the windy storm and tempest
Have I found my rest.

Learning from Thy lips for ever
All the Father's heart,
Thou hast, in that joy eternal,
Chosen me my part.

There, where Jesus, Jesus only,
Fills each heart and tongue,
Where Himself is all the radiance
And Himself the song.

Here, who follows Him the nearest,
Needs must walk alone;
There like many seas the chorus,
Praise surrounds the throne.

Here a dark and silent pathway;
In those courts so fair
Countless hosts, yet each beholding
Jesus only, there.

—"T. P."

THEE WILL I LOVE

Thee will I love, my Strength, my Tower,
Thee will I love, my Joy, my Crown,
Thee will I love with all my power,
In all Thy works, and Thee alone;
Thee will I love, till the pure fire
Fill my whole soul with chaste desire.

Ah, why did I so late Thee know,
Thee, lovelier than the sons of men!
Ah, why did I no sooner go
To Thee, the only ease in pain!
Ashamed, I sigh, and inly mourn,
That I so late to Thee did turn.

I thank Thee, uncreated Sun,
That Thy bright beams on me have shined;
I thank Thee, who hast overthrown
My foes, and healed my wounded mind;
I thank Thee, whose enlivening voice
Bids my freed heart in Thee rejoice.

Uphold me in the doubtful race,
Nor suffer me again to stray;
Strengthen my feet with steady pace
Still to press forward in Thy way;
My soul and flesh, O Lord of might,
Fill, satiate, with Thy heavenly light.

Give to mine eyes refreshing tears,
Give to my heart chaste, hallowed fires,
Give to my soul, with filial fires,
The love that all heaven's host inspires;
That all my powers, with all their might,
In Thy sole glory may unite.

Thee will I love, my Joy, my Crown,
Thee will I love, my Lord, my God;
Thee will I love, beneath Thy frown,
Or smile, Thy sceptre, or Thy rod;
What though my flesh and heart decay,
Thee shall I love in endless day.

—JOHANN SCHEFFLER, 1624-1677
Tr. John Wesley, 1703-1791

AT THE LORD'S TABLE

Here, O my Lord, I see Thee face to face;
Here would I touch and handle things unseen,
Here grasp with firmer hand the eternal grace,
And all my weariness upon Thee lean.

Here would I feed upon the bread of God,
Here drink with Thee the royal wine of heaven;
Here would I lay aside each earthly load,
Here taste afresh the calm of sin forgiven.

This is the hour of banquet and of song;
This is the heavenly table spread for me;
Here let me feast, and feasting, still prolong
The brief bright hour of fellowship with Thee.

Too soon we rise; the symbols disappear;
The feast, though not the love, is past and gone;
The bread and wine remove, but Thou art here,
Nearer than ever; still my Shield and Sun.

I have no help but Thine; nor do I need
Another arm save Thine to lean upon;
It is enough, my Lord, enough indeed;
My strength is in Thy might, Thy might alone.

Mine is the sin, but Thine the righteousness;
Mine is the guilt, but Thine the cleansing blood;
Here is my robe, my refuge, and my peace, —
Thy blood, Thy righteousness, O Lord my God.

Feast after feast thus comes and passes by,
Yet, passing, points to the glad feast above,
Giving sweet foretaste of the festal joy,
The Lamb's great bridal feast of bliss and love.

—HORATIUS BONAR, 1808-1889

PRAYER BEFORE COMMUNION

Bread of the world, in mercy broken,
Wine of the soul, in mercy shed,
By whom the words of life were spoken,
And in whose death our sins are dead:
Look on the heart by sorrow broken,
Look on the tears by sinners shed;
And be Thy feast to us the token
That by Thy grace our souls are fed.

—REGINALD HEBER, 1783-1826

THE INDWELLING CHRIST

Thou who givest of Thy gladness
Till the cup runs o'er—
Cup whereof the pilgrim weary
Drinks to thirst no more—
Not a-nigh me, but within me
Is Thy joy divine;
Thou, O Lord, hast made Thy dwelling
In this heart of mine.

Need I that a law should bind me
Captive unto Thee?
Captive is my heart, rejoicing
Never to be free.
Ever with me, glorious, awful,
Tender, passing sweet,
One upon whose heart I rest me,
Worship at His Feet.

With me, wheresoe'er I wander,
That great Presence goes,
That unutterable gladness,
Undisturbed repose.
Everywhere the blessed stillness
Of His Holy Place—
Stillness of the love that worships
Dumb before His Face.

To Thy house, O God my Father,
Thy lost child is come;
Led by wandering lights no longer,
I have found my home.
Over moor and fen I tracked them
Through the midnight blast,
But to find the Light eternal
In my heart at last.

—GERHARD TERSTEEGEN, 1697-1769
Tr. Unknown

AS INCENSE STREAMING FORTH

Thy Name, O Christ, as incense streaming forth
Sweetens our names before God's Holy Face;
Luring us from the south and from the north
Unto the sacred place.

In Thee God's promise is Amen and Yea.
What art Thou to us? Prize of every lot,
Shepherd and Door, our Life and Truth and Way:—
Nay, Lord, what art Thou not?

—CHRISTINA ROSSETTI, 1830-1894

HOSANNA, LORD!

Hosanna to the living Lord!
Hosanna to th' incarnate Word!
To Christ, Creator, Saviour, King,
Let earth, let heaven, Hosanna sing!

Hosanna, Lord! Thine angels cry;
Hosanna, Lord! Thy saints reply;
Above, beneath us, and around,
The dead and living swell the sound.

O Saviour, with protecting care,
Return to this Thy house of prayer:
Where we Thy parting promise claim:
Assembled in Thy sacred Name.

But, chiefest, in our cleansed breast,
Eternal! bid Thy Spirit rest;
And make our secret soul to be
A temple pure, and worthy Thee.

So in the last and dreadful day,
When earth and heaven shall melt away,
Thy flock, redeemed from sinful stain,
Shall swell the sound of praise again.

—REGINALD HEBER, 1783-1826

AM I NOT ENOUGH?

Am I not enough, Mine own? enough,
Mine own, for thee?
Hath the world its palace towers,
Garden glades of magic flowers,
Where thou fain wouldst be?
Fair things and false are there,
False things but fair.
All shalt thou find at last,
Only in Me.
Am I not enough, Mine own? I, for ever
and alone, I, needing thee?

—*GERHARD TERSTEEGEN, 1697-1769*
Tr. Unknown

JESUS, THOU JOY OF LOVING HEARTS

Jesus, Thou Joy of loving hearts,
Thou Fount of life, Thou Light of men,
From the best bliss that earth imparts
We turn unfilled to Thee again.

Thy truth unchanged hath ever stood;
Thou savest those that on Thee call:
To them that seek Thee Thou art good,
To them that find Thee, all in all.

We taste Thee, O Thou living Bread,
And long to feast upon Thee still;
We drink of Thee, the Fountain-head,
And thirst our souls from Thee to fill.

Our restless spirits yearn for Thee,
Where'er our changeful lot is cast, —
Glad when Thy gracious smile we see,
Blest when our faith can hold Thee fast.

O Jesus, ever with us stay;
Make all our moments calm and bright;
Chase the dark night of sin away;
Shed o'er the world Thy holy light.

—BERNARD OF CLAIRVAUX, 1091-1153
Tr. Ray Palmer, 1808-1887

Joyous Anticipation of Christ's Return

WAKE, AWAKE, FOR NIGHT IS FLYING

"Wake, awake, for night is flying,"
The watchmen on the heights are crying;
"Awake, Jerusalem, at last!"
Midnight hears the welcome voices,
And at the thrilling cry rejoices:
"Come forth, ye virgins, night is past!
The Bride-groom comes, awake,
Your lamps with gladness take;
Hallelujah!
And for His marriage feast prepare,
For ye must go to meet Him there."

Zion hears the watchmen singing,
And all her heart with joy is springing;
She wakes, she rises from her gloom;
For her Lord comes down all glorious,
The strong in grace, in truth victorious,
Her Star is risen, her Light is come!
Ah come, Thou blessed Lord,
O Jesus, Son of God,
Hallelujah!
We follow till the halls we see
Where Thou hast bid us sup with Thee.

Now let all the heavens adore Thee,
And men and angels sing before Thee,
With harp and cymbal's clearest tone;
Of one pearl each shining portal,
Where we are with the choir immortal
Of angels round Thy dazzling throne;
Nor eye bath seen, nor ear
Hath yet attained to hear,
What there is ours;
But we rejoice, and sing to Thee
Our hymns of joy eternally.

—PHILIPP NICOLAI, 1556-1608
Tr. Catherine Winkworth, 1829-1878

LO! HE COMES!

Lo! He comes, with clouds descending,
Once for favored sinners slain:
Thousand thousand saints attending,
Swell the triumph of His train:
Hallelujah!
God appears on earth to reign!

See the universe in motion,
Sinking on her funeral pyre—
Earth dissolving, and the ocean
Vanishing in final fire:
Hark the trumpet!
Loud proclaims the Day of Ire!

Graves have yawned in countless numbers,
From the dust the dead arise;
Millions out of silent slumbers,
Wake in overwhelmed surprise;
Where creation
Wrecked and torn on ruin lies!

See the Judge our nature wearing,
Pure, ineffable, divine:

See the great Archangel bearing
High in heaven the mystic sign:
Cross of Glory!
Christ be in that moment mine!

Every eye shall now behold Him
Robed in dreadful majesty;
Those who set aside and sold Him,
Pierced and nailed Him to the tree,
Deeply wailing,
Shall the true Messiah see.

All the tokens of His passion
Still His dazzling body bears;
Cause of endless exultation
To His ransomed worshippers;
With what rapture
Gaze we on those glorious scars.

Lo! the last long separation!
As the cleaving crowds divide;
And one dread adjudication
Sends each soul to either side!
Lord of mercy!
How shall I that day abide!

O, may Thine own Bride and Spirit
Then avert a dreadful doom,
And me summon to inherit
An eternal blissful home:—
Ah! come quickly!
Let Thy second advent come!

Yea, Amen! Let all adore Thee
High on Thine eternal throne!
Saviour—take the power and glory;
Make Thy righteous sentence known:
Jah! Jehovah!
Claim the kingdom for Thine own.

—JOHN CENNICK, et al. 1718-1755

THE HOPE OF HIS COMING

There is a balm for every pain,
A medicine for all sorrow;
The eye turned backward to the Cross,
And forward to the morrow.

The morrow of the glory and the psalm,
When He shall come;
The morrow of the harping and the palm,
The welcome home.
Meantime in His beloved hands our ways,
And on His Heart the wandering heart at rest;
And comfort for the weary one who lays
His head upon His Breast.

—GERHARD TERSTEEGEN, 1697-1769
Tr. Unknown

THE BLESSED MORROW

'Midst the darkness, storm, and sorrow,
One bright gleam I see;
Well I know the blessed morrow
Christ will come for me.
'Midst the light, and peace, and glory
Of the Father's home,
Christ for me is watching, waiting,
Waiting till I come.

Long the blessed Guide has led me
By the desert road;
Now I see the golden towers,
City of my God.
There, amidst the love and glory,
He is waiting yet;
On His hands a name is graven
He can ne'er forget.

There, amidst the songs of heaven,
Sweeter to His ear
Is the footfall through the desert,
Ever drawing near.
There, made ready are the mansions,
Radiant, still, and fair;
But the Bride the Father gave Him
Yet is wanting there.

Who is this who comes to meet me
On the desert way,
As the Morning Star foretelling
God's unclouded day?
He it is who came to win me
On the Cross of shame;
In His glory well I know Him
Evermore the same.

Oh the blessed joy of meeting,
All the desert past!
Oh the wondrous words of greeting
He shall speak at last!
He and I together entering
Those fair courts above—
He and I together sharing
All the Father's love.

Where no shade nor stain can enter,
Nor the gold be dim,
In that holiness unsullied,
I shall walk with Him.
Meet companion then for Jesus,
From Him, for Him, made—
Glory of God's grace for ever
There in me displayed.

He who in His hour of sorrow
Bore the curse alone;
I who through the lonely desert
Trod where He had gone;
He and I, in that bright glory,
One deep joy shall share—
Mine, to be for ever with Him;
His, that I am there.

—GERHARD TERSTEEGEN, 1697-1769
Tr. Unknown

IMMORTALITY AND THE WORLD TO COME

LIFT YOUR GLAD VOICES

Lift your glad voices in triumph on high,
For Jesus hath risen, and man cannot die.
Vain were the terrors that gathered around Him,
And short the dominion of death and the grave;
He burst from the fetters of darkness that bound Him,
Resplendent in glory, to live and to save.
Loud was the chorus of angels on high, —
"The Saviour hath risen, and man shall not die."

Glory to God, in full anthems of joy;
The being He gave us, death cannot destroy.
Sad were the life we must part with tomorrow,
If tears were our birthright, and death were our end;
But Jesus hath cheered the dark valley of sorrow,
And bade us, immortal, to heaven ascend.
Lift, then, your voices in triumph on high,
For Jesus hath risen, and man shall not die.

—HENRY WARE, 1794-1843

JESUS LIVES, AND SO SHALL I

Jesus lives, and so shall I.
Death! thy sting is gone forever:
He, who deigned for me to die,

Lives, the bands of death to sever.
He shall raise me with the just:
Jesus is my Hope and Trust.

Jesus lives and reigns supreme;
And, His kingdom still remaining,
I shall also be with Him,
Ever living, ever reigning.
God has promised; be it must:
Jesus is my Hope and Trust.

Jesus lives, and God extends
Grace to each returning sinner;
Rebels He receives as friends,
And exalts to highest honor.
God is True as He is Just;
Jesus is my Hope and Trust.

Jesus lives, and by His grace,
Victory o'er my passions giving,
I will cleanse my heart and ways,
Ever to His glory living.
The weak He raises from the dust:
Jesus is my Hope and Trust.

Jesus lives, and I am sure
Naught shall e'er from Jesus sever,
Satan's wiles, and Satan's power,
Pain or pleasure—ye shall never!
Christian armor can not rust:
Jesus is my Hope and Trust.

Jesus lives, and death is now
But my entrance into glory.
Courage! then, my soul, for thou
Hast a crown of life before thee;
Thou shalt find thy hopes were just—
Jesus is the Christian's Trust.

—CHRISTIAN F. GELLERT, 1715-1769
Tr. Unknown

O SING HALLELUJAH!

Our Lord Christ hath risen!
The tempter is foiled;
His legions are scattered,
His strongholds are spoiled.
O sing Hallelujah! O sing Hallelujah!
O sing Hallelujah, be joyful and sing,
Our great foe is baffled—Christ Jesus is King!

O sin, thou art vanquished,
Thy long reign is o'er;
Though still thou dost vex us,
We dread thee no more.
O sing Hallelujah! O sing Hallelujah!
O sing Hallelujah, be joyful and sing,
Who now can condemn us? Christ Jesus is King!

O death we defy thee!
A stronger than thou
Hath entered thy palace;
We fear thee not now!
O sing Hallelujah! O sing Hallelujah!
O sing Hallelujah, be joyful and sing,
The grave cannot scare us—Christ Jesus is King!

Our Lord Christ hath risen!
Day breaketh at last;
The long night of weeping
Is now well-nigh past.
O sing Hallelujah! O sing Hallelujah!
O sing Hallelujah, be joyful and sing,
Our foes are all conquered—Christ Jesus is King!

—*LORD PLUNKET—BISHOP OF MEATH, 1629-1681*

THOSE ENDLESS SABBATHS

O what their joy and their glory must be,
Those endless Sabbaths the blessed ones see!
Crown for the valiant; to weary ones rest;
God shall be all, and in all ever blest.

What are the Monarch, His court, and His throne?
What are the peace and the joy that they own?
Tell us, ye blest ones, that in it have share,
If what ye feel ye can fully declare.

Truly Jerusalem name we that shore,
"Vision of peace," that brings joy evermore!
Wish and fulfilment can severed be ne'er,
Nor the thing prayed for come short of the prayer.

We, where no trouble distraction can bring,
Safely the anthems of Zion shall sing;
While for Thy grace, Lord, their voices of praise
Thy blessed people shall evermore raise.

Low before Him with our praises we fall,
Of whom, and in whom, and through whom are all;
Of whom, the Father; and through whom, the Son;
In whom, the Spirit, with these ever One.

—*PIERRE ABELARD, 1079-1142*
Tr. John Mason Neale, 1818-1866

IN IMMANUEL'S LAND

The sands of time are sinking,
The dawn of Heaven breaks,
The summer morn I've sighed for,
The fair sweet morn awakes:
Dark, dark hath been the midnight,
But dayspring is at hand,
And glory—glory dwelleth
In Immanuel's land.

Oh! well it is for ever,
Oh! well for evermore,
My nest hung in no forest
Of all this death-doom'd shore:
Yea, let the vain world vanish,
As from the ship the strand,
While glory—glory dwelleth
In Immanuel's land.

There the Red Rose of Sharon
Unfolds its heartsome bloom,
And fills the air of Heaven
With ravishing perfume:—
Oh! to behold it blossom,
While by its fragrance farm'd
Where glory—glory dwelleth
In Immanuel's land.

The King there in His beauty,
Without a veil, is seen:
It were a well-spent journey,
Though seven deaths lay between.
The Lamb, with His fair army,
Doth on Mount Zion stand,
And glory—glory dwelleth
In Immanuel's land.

Oh! Christ He is the Fountain,
The deep sweet well of love!
The streams on earth I've tasted,
More deep I'll drink above:
There, to an ocean fulness,
His mercy doth expand,
And glory—glory dwelleth
In Immanuel's land.

E'en Anwoth was not heaven—
E'en preaching was not Christ;
And in my sea-beat prison
My Lord and I held tryst:
And aye my murkiest storm-cloud
Was by a rainbow spann'd,

Caught from the glory dwelling
In Immanuel's land.

But that He built a heaven
Of His surpassing love,
A little New Jerusalem,
Like to the one above,—
"Lord, take me o'er the water,"
Had been my loud demand,
"Take me to love's own country,
Unto Immanuel's land."

But flowers need night's cool darkness
The moonlight and the dew;
So Christ, from one who loved it,
His shining oft withdrew;
And then for cause of absence,
My troubled soul I scann'd—
But glory, shadeless, shineth
In Immanuel's land.

The little birds of Anwoth
I used to count them blest,—
Now, beside happier altars
I go to build my nest:
O'er these there broods no silence,
No graves around them stand,
For glory, deathless, dwelleth
In Immanuel's land.

Fair Anwoth by the Solway,
To me thou still art dear!
E'en from the verge of Heaven
I drop for thee a tear.
Oh! if one soul from Anwoth
Meet me at God's right hand,
My Heaven will be two Heavens,
In Immanuel's land.

I have wrestled on toward Heaven,
'Gainst storm, and wind, and tide:—
Now, like a weary traveller,

That leaneth on his guide,
Amid the shades of evening,
While sinks life's ling'ring sand,
I hail the glory dawning
From Immanuel's land.

Deep water cross'd life's pathway,
The hedge of thorns was sharp;
Now these lie all behind me—
Oh! for a well-tuned harp!
Oh! to join Hallelujah
With yon triumphant band,
Who sing, where glory dwelleth,
In Immanuel's land.

With mercy and with judgment
My web of time He wove,
And aye the dews of sorrow
Were lustered with His love.
I'll bless the hand that guided,
I'll bless the heart that plann'd,
When throned where glory dwelleth
In Immanuel's land.

Soon shall the cup of glory
Wash down earth's bitterest woes,
Soon shall the desert-briar
Break into Eden's rose:
The curse shall change to blessing—
The name on earth that's bann'd,
Be graven on the white stone
In Immanuel's land.
Oh! I am my Beloved's,
And my Beloved is mine!
He brings a poor vile sinner
Into His "House of wine."
I stand upon His merit,
I know no other stand,
Not e'en where glory dwelleth
In Immanuel's land.

I shall sleep sound in Jesus,
Fill'd with His likeness rise,
To live and to adore Him,
To see Him with these eyes
'Tween me and resurrection
But Paradise doth stand;
Then—then for glory dwelling
In Immanuel's land!

The Bride eyes not her garment,
But her dear Bridegroom's face;
I will not gaze at glory,
But on my King of Grace—
Not at the crown He giveth,
But on His pierced hand:
The Lamb is all the glory
Of Immanuel's land.

I have borne scorn and hatred,
I have borne wrong and shame,
Earth's proud ones have reproach'd me,
For Christ's thrice blessed name:—
Where God His seal set fairest
They've stamp'd their foulest brand;
But judgment shines like noonday
In Immanuel's land.

They've summoned me before them,
But there I may not come,—
My Lord says, "Come up hither,"
My Lord says, "Welcome Home!"
My kingly King, at His white throne,
My presence cloth command,
Where glory—glory dwelleth
In Immanuel's land.

—*ANNE R. COUSIN, 1824-1906*

THE CELESTIAL COUNTRY

The world is very evil,
The times are waxing late;
Be sober and keep vigil,
The Judge is at the gate—
The Judge that comes in mercy,
The Judge that comes with might,
To terminate the evil,
To diadem the right.
When the just and gentle Monarch
Shall summon from the tomb,
Let man, the guilty, tremble,
For Man, the God, shall doom!

Arise, arise, good Christian,
Let right to wrong succeed;
Let penitential sorrow
To heavenly gladness lead—
To the light that hath no evening,
That knows nor moon nor sun,
The light so new and golden,
The light that is but one.

And when the Sole-Begotten
Shall render up once more
The kingdom to the Father,
Whose own it was before,
Then glory yet unheard of
Shall shed abroad its ray,
Resolving all enigmas,
An endless Sabbath-day.

Then, then from his oppressors
The Hebrew shall go free,
And celebrate in triumph
The year of jubilee;
And the sunlit Land that recks not
Of tempest nor of fight,
Shall fold within its bosom
Each happy Israelite—
The Home of fadeless splendor,

Of flowers that fear no thorn,
Where they shall dwell as children,
Who here as exiles mourn.

Midst power that knows no limit,
And wisdom free from bound,
The Beatific Vision
Shall glad the Saints around—
The peace of all the faithful,
The calm of all the blest,
Inviolate, unvaried,
Divinest, sweetest, best.
Yes, peace! for war is needless—
Yes, calm! for storm is past—
And goal from finished labor,
And anchorage at last.

That peace—but who may claim it?
The guileless in their way,
Who keep the ranks of battle,
Who mean the thing they say—
The peace that is for heaven,
And shall be for the earth;
The palace that re-echoes
With festal song and mirth;
The garden, breathing spices,
The paradise on high;
Grace beautified to glory,
Unceasing minstrelsy.

There nothing can be feeble,
There none can ever mourn,
There nothing is divided,
There nothing can be torn.
'Tis fury, ill, and scandal,
'Tis peaceless peace below;
Peace, endless, strifeless, ageless,
The halls of Syon know.

O happy, holy portion,
Refection for the blest,
True vision of true beauty,

Sweet cure of all distrest!
Strive, man, to win that glory;
Toil, man, to gain that light;
Send hope before to grasp it,
Till hope be lost in sight;
Till Jesus gives the portion
Those blessed souls to fill—
The insatiate, yet satisfied,
The full, yet craving still.

That fulness and that craving
Alike are free from pain,
Where thou, midst heavenly citizens,
A home like theirs shalt gain.
Here is the warlike trumpet;
There, life set free from sin,
When to the last Great Supper
The faithful shall come in;
When the heavenly net is laden
With fishes many and great
(So glorious in its fulness,
Yet so inviolate);
And perfect from unperfected,
And fall'n from those that stand,
And the sheep-flock from the goat-herd
Shall part on either hand.

And these shall pass to torment,
And those shall triumph then—
The new peculiar nation,
Blest number of blest men.
Jerusalem demands them;
They paid the price on earth,
And now shall reap the harvest
In blissfulness and mirth—
The glorious holy people,
Who evermore relied
Upon their Chief and Father,
The King, the Crucified—
The sacred ransomed number
Now bright with endless sheen,
Who made the Cross their watchword

Of Jesus Nazarene,
Who (fed with heavenly nectar
Where soul-like odors play)
Draw out the endless leisure
Of that long vernal day.

And, through the sacred lilies
And flowers on every side,
The happy dear-bought people
Go wandering far and wide;
Their breasts are filled with gladness,
Their mouths are tun'd to praise,
What time, now safe for ever,
On former sins they gaze:
The fouler was the error,
The sadder was the fall,
The ampler are the praises
Of Him who pardoned all.

Their one and only anthem,
The fulness of His love,
Who gives instead of torment,
Eternal joys above—
Instead of torment, glory;
Instead of death, that life
Wherewith your happy Country,
True Israelites, is rife.
Brief life is here our portion,
Brief sorrow, short-liv'd care;
The life that knows no ending—
The tearless life, is there.

O happy retribution!
Short toil, eternal rest;
For mortals and for sinners
A mansion with the blest!
That we should look, poor wand'rers,
To have our home on high!
That worms should seek for dwelling,
Beyond the starry sky!
To all one happy guerdon
Of one celestial grace;

For all, for all, who mourn their fall,
Is one eternal place.

And martyrdom hath roses
Upon that heavenly ground;
And white and virgin lilies
For virgin-souls abound.
There grief is turned to pleasure—
Such pleasure as below
No human voice can utter,
No human heart can know;
And after fleshly scandal,
And after this world's night,
And after storm and whirlwind,
Is calm, and joy, and light.

And now we fight the battle,
But then shall wear the crown
Of full and everlasting
And passionless renown:
And now we watch and struggle,
And now we live in hope,
And Syon, in her anguish,
With Babylon must cope;
But He whom now we trust in
Shall then be seen and known,
And they that know and see Him
Shall have Him for their own.

The miserable pleasures
Of the body shall decay;
The bland and flattering struggles
Of the flesh shall pass away;
And none shall there be jealous,
And none shall there contend;
Fraud, clamor, guile—what say I?
All ill, all ill shall end!
And there is David's Fountain,
And life in fullest glow;
And there the light is golden,
And milk and honey flow—
The light that hath no evening,

The health that hath no sore,
The life that hath no ending,
But lasteth evermore.

There Jesus shall embrace us,
There Jesus be embraced—
That spirit's food and sunshine
Whence earthly love is chased.
Amidst the happy chorus,
A place, however low,
Shall shew Him us, and shewing,
Shall satiate evermo.

By hope we struggle onward:
While here we must be fed
By milk, as tender infants,
But there by Living Bread.
The night was full of terror,
The morn is bright with gladness;
The Cross becomes our harbor,
And we triumph after sadness.

And Jesus to His true ones
Brings trophies fair to see;
And Jesus shall be loved, and
Beheld in Galilee—
Beheld, when morn shall waken,
And shadows shall decay,
And each true-hearted servant
Shall shine as doth the day;
And every ear shall hear it—
"Behold thy King's array,
Behold thy God in beauty,
The Law hath pass'd away!"
Yes! God my King and Portion,
In fulness of Thy grace,
We then shall see for ever,
And worship face to face.
Then Jacob into Israel,
From earthlier self estranged,
And Leah into Rachel
For ever shall be changed;

Then all the halls of Syon
For aye shall be complete,
And in the Land of Beauty,
All things of beauty meet.

For thee, O dear, dear Country!
Mine eyes their vigils keep;
For very love, beholding
Thy happy name, they weep.
The mention of thy glory
Is unction to the breast,
And medicine in sickness,
and love, and life, and rest.
O One, O only Mansion!
O Paradise of Joy!
Where tears are ever banished,
And smiles have no alloy,
Beside thy living waters
All plants are, great and small,
The cedar of the forest,
The hyssop of the wall;
With jaspers glow thy bulwarks,
Thy streets with emeralds blaze,
The sardius and the topaz
Unite in thee their rays;
Thine ageless walls are bonded
With amethyst unpriced;
Thy Saints build up its fabric,
And the corner-stone is Christ.

The Cross is all thy splendor,
The Crucified thy praise;
His laud and benediction
Thy ransomed people raise:
"Jesus, the Gem of Beauty,
True God and Man," they sing,
"The never-failing Garden,
The ever-golden Ring;
The Door, the Pledge, the Husband,
The Guardian of his Court;
The Day-star of Salvation,
The Porter and the Port!"

Thou hast no shore, fair ocean!
Thou hast no time, bright day!
Dear fountain of refreshment
To pilgrims far away!
Upon the Rock of Ages
They raise thy holy tower;
Thine is the victor's laurel,
And thine the golden dower!
Thou feel'st in mystic rapture,
O Bride that know'st no guile,
The Prince's sweetest kisses,
The Prince's loveliest smile;
Unfading lilies, bracelets
Of living pearl thine own;
The Lamb is ever near thee,
The Bridegroom thine alone.
The Crown is He to guerdon,
The Buckler to protect,
And he Himself the Mansion,
And He the Architect.

The only art thou needest—
Thanksgiving for thy lot;
The only joy thou seekest—
The Life where Death is not.
And all thine endless leisure,
In sweetest accents, sings
The ill that was thy merit,
The wealth that is thy King's!

Jerusalem the golden,
With milk and honey blest,
Beneath thy contemplation
Sink heart and voice oppressed.
I know not, O I know not,
What social joys are there!
What radiancy of glory,
What light beyond compare!

And when I fain would sing them,
My spirit fails and faints;
And vainly would it image

The assembly of the Saints.
They stand, those halls of Syon,
Conjubilant with song,
And bright with many an angel,
And all the martyr throng;
The Prince is ever in them,
The daylight is serene;
The pastures of the Blessed
Are decked in glorious sheen.

There is the Throne of David,
And there, from care released,
The song of them that triumph,
The shout of them that feast;
And they who, with their Leader,
Have conquered in the fight,
For ever and for ever
Are clad in robes of white!

O holy, placid harp-notes
Of that eternal hymn!
O sacred, sweet refection,
And peace of Seraphim!
O thirst, for ever ardent,
Yet evermore content!
O true peculiar vision
Of God cunctipotent!
Ye know the many mansions
For many a glorious name,
And divers retributions
That divers merits claim;
For midst the constellations
That deck our earthly sky,
This star than that is brighter—
And so it is on high.
Jerusalem the glorious!
The glory of the Elect!
O dear and future vision
That eager hearts expect!
Even now by faith I see thee,
Even here thy walls discern;
To thee my thoughts are kindled,

And strive, and pant, and yearn.

Jerusalem the only,
That look'st from heaven below,
In thee is all my glory,
In me is all my woe;
And though my body may not,
My spirit seeks thee fain,
Till flesh and earth return me
To earth and flesh again.

O none can tell thy bulwarks,
How gloriously they rise!
O none can tell thy capitals
O beautiful device!
Thy loveliness oppresses
All human thought and heart;
And none, O peace, O Syon,
Can sing thee as thou art!

New mansion of new people,
Whom God's own love and light
Promote, increase, make holy,
Identify, unite!
Thou City of the Angels!
Thou City of the Lord!
Whose everlasting music
Is the glorious decachord!

And there the band of Prophets
United praise ascribes,
And there the twelvefold chorus
Of Israel's ransomed tribes,
The lily-beds of virgins,
The roses' martyr-glow,
The cohort of the Fathers
Who kept the Faith below.

And there the Sole-Begotten
Is Lord in regal state—
He, Judah's mystic Lion,
He, Lamb Immaculate.

O fields that know no sorrow!
O state that fears no strife!
O princely bowers! O land of flowers!
O realm and home of Life!

Jerusalem, exulting
On that securest shore,
I hope thee, wish thee, sing thee,
And love thee evermore!
I ask not for my merit,
I seek not to deny
My merit is destruction,
A child of wrath am I;
But yet with Faith I venture
And Hope upon my way;
For those perennial guerdons
I labor night and day.

The best and dearest Father,
Who made me and who saved,
Bore with me in defilement,
And from defilement laved,
When in His strength I struggle,
For very joy I leap,

When in my sin I totter,
I weep, or try to weep:
But grace, sweet grace celestial,
Shall all its love display,
And David's Royal Fountain
Purge every sin away.

O mine, my golden Syon!
O lovelier far than gold,
With laurel-girt battalions,
And safe victorious fold!
O sweet and blessed Country,
Shall I ever see thy face?
O sweet and blessed Country,
Shall I ever win thy grace?
I have the hope within me
To comfort and to bless!

Shall I ever win the prize itself?
O tell me, tell me, Yes!

Exult, O dust and ashes!
The Lord shall be thy part;
His only, His for ever,
Thou shalt be, and thou art!
Exult, O dust and ashes!
The Lord shall be thy part;
His only, His for ever,
Thou shalt be, and thou art!

—BERNARD OF CLUNY, 12th Century

Notes

1. This hymn dates from the fourth century and is generally acknowledged to be one of the greatest ever written.

   As a night bird sings out of the darkness and we hear its song without locating its exact source, so the Te Deum sings out of the obscurity of the past. The author is not certainly known. Some have attributed the hymn to Ambrose, Bishop of Milan, but the weight of scholarly opinion would favor Nicetas, Bishop of Remesiana in Dacia.

   Whoever composed it, one thing is certain: it has through the centuries been for countless thousands of Christians a ringing affirmation of faith in God and an expression of complete confidence in Jesus Christ His Son. Here are found also confession of sin, ecstatic praise and a tender plea for mercy. Altogether it is theology aflame with devotion, and this we believe is an offering well pleasing to God.

2. This much-loved poem was composed by Mrs. Anne Ross Cousin, wife of a minister of the Free Church of Scotland. The poem is as remarkable as it is beautiful in that Mrs. Cousin extracted from the letters of Samuel Rutherford many of his most memorable sayings and wove them into a hymn of nineteen stanzas, maintaining throughout high poetic excellence and great faithfulness to the language and spirit of the letters.

   Certain stanzas of this poem are familiar to most Christians as "The Sands of Time Are Sinking."

3. Bernard of Cluny was born, probably of English parents, either at Morlaix (Brittany), or at Morlas, in the Pyrenees. Neither the exact time and place of his birth nor the date of his death is known with certainty.

   Bernard joined the Benedictine order and entered the Abbey of Cluny, in northern France. There about A. D. 1145 he wrote De Contemptu Mundi, a bold and merciless attack upon the moral and spiritual corruption of the world as found in society generally and in the Roman Church in particular. The outraged prophet spared nothing and no one, from the Pope down, but in words of burning eloquence set forth count after count in a terrible indictment of the Church as well as of the world. The whole long poem consists of about 3,000 lines.

About a hundred years ago Dr. John Mason Neale, the celebrated English scholar and linguist, turned a part of Bernard's poem into English verse. This work appears here under the title "The Celestial Country." It is my opinion that nothing in the English language remotely compares with this in its beautiful sorrow for earth and its rapturous description of heaven.

Here time and eternity are blended as the grief-stricken but enraptured monk shows us the ugliness of earth and the loveliness of heaven. As time fades away, eternity rises to gather all redeemed and blood-washed souls in an everlasting embrace of pure and perfect love. Here we find the triumphant answer to all questions concerning the chief end of man. Bernard knew the answer, and so do all who read sympathetically his lovely and inspired poem.

www.ingramcontent.com/pod-product-compliance
Lightning Source LLC
Chambersburg PA
CBHW030231100526
44583CB00013BA/878